BLACKBIRDS SINGING

Also by Janet Dewart Bell

Lighting the Fires of Freedom: African American Women in the Civil Rights Movement

Race, Rights, and Redemption: The Derrick Bell Lectures on the Law and Critical Race Theory
(co-edited with Vincent M. Southerland)

BLACKBIRDS SINGING

INSPIRING BLACK WOMEN'S SPEECHES FROM THE CIVIL WAR TO THE TWENTY-FIRST CENTURY

JANET DEWART BELL, PHD

NEW YORK
LONDON

See page 299 for additional permissions information.

Published in the United States by The New Press, New York, 2024
Distributed by Two Rivers Distribution

ISBN 978-1-62097-628-9 (hc)
ISBN 978-1-62097-629-6 (ebook)
CIP data is available

The New Press publishes books that promote and enrich public discussion and understanding of the issues vital to our democracy and to a more equitable world. These books are made possible by the enthusiasm of our readers; the support of a committed group of donors, large and small; the collaboration of our many partners in the independent media and the not-for-profit sector; booksellers, who often hand-sell New Press books; librarians; and above all by our authors.

www.thenewpress.com

Book design and composition by Bookbright Media
This book was set in Adobe Caslon, Bodoni 72, and Texta

Printed in the United States of America

10 9 8 7 6 5 4 3 2 1

To my mother,
Willie Mae Neal,
whose life was a song of compassion and love

CONTENTS

INTRODUCTION

In their October 7, 2020, debate, when then senator and vice presidential candidate Kamala Harris emphatically said, "I'm speaking, Mr. Vice President" to Mike Pence, her statement was more than a reaction to his chauvinism and "mansplaining." What she said resonated with women who have been cut off, but especially with African American women, who have experienced it all before—and have been fighting to be heard since their enslavement in this country.

Blackbirds Singing contains speeches and quotations from African American women in the context of the struggle for freedom and social justice. Because Black women were prohibited and then inhibited from being involved in the political system, the book expands the definition of speeches to include some writings that women did not have the opportunity to present in a public forum.

Even as Black women negotiated or forced our way into the public square, our words were often distorted and taken out of context or simply ignored. Because we did not own the means of communications—from printing presses to the internet, Black women often talked into the wind. But somehow, some remarkable women were able to have their say. This book is about them and what they said. It is also about their courage in speaking up and speaking out. Their words—powerful and prophetic.

And while Amanda Gorman may not have had the words of these foremothers in mind when she wrote her 2020 inaugural poem, "The Hill We Climb," she captured their spirit and legacy. From the darkest hours, Black women saw the light and led it into existence:

The new dawn blooms as we free it
For there is always light,
if only we're brave enough to see it
If only we're brave enough to be it

With the exception of minor typographical corrections, all of the speeches in this volume appear in their original form, including phrasing and usage as determined by their authors.

BLACKBIRDS SINGING

1

Sojourner Truth

1797–1883

Sojourner Truth's life span and experiences covered an extraordinary period in the life of America—slavery, the Civil War, emancipation, and the beginning of the fight for women's suffrage. She was a woman of her time and greater than her time, whose vision, determination, and courage constantly challenged systems of injustice and broke boundaries.

When Isabella ran away from her slave master, she had time to gather only one child, her daughter, and had to leave behind her son. The reality is that the brutal institution of American chattel slavery could separate her from her children at any time, without remorse and without consequences. Black family separation was not an aberration but a cruelty codified in custom and in law; its insidious consequences resonate in our nation today. Not one to give up, Isabella successfully sued to get back her son. And incredibly "became the first black woman to win such a case against a white man" (sojournertruthmemorial.org).

Unable to read and write, Isabella had a phenomenal memory and gave powerful speeches—so memorable that even without the benefit of wealth and the support of contemporary biographers, her work and speeches have withstood the test of time. After the end of the Civil War, she also taught at the Freedman's Village, the later site of Arlington National Cemetery.

Isabella reinvented her life, in fact gave herself new life as an itinerant wanderer who spoke truth to power. She became Sojourner Truth.

Address to the First Annual Meeting of the American Equal Rights Association

May 9, 1867, New York, New York

My friends, I am rejoiced that you are glad, but I don't know how you will feel when I get through. I come from another field—the country of the slave. They have got their liberty—so much good luck to have slavery partly destroyed; not entirely. I want it root and branch destroyed. Then we will all be free indeed. I feel that if I have to answer for the deeds done in my body just as much as a man, I have a right to have just as much as a man.

There is a great stir about colored men getting their rights, but not a word about the colored women; and if colored men get their rights, and not colored women theirs, you see the colored men will be masters over the women, and it will be just as bad as it was before. So I am for keeping the thing going while things are stirring; because if we wait till it is still, it will take a great while to get it going again. White women are a great deal smarter, and know more than colored women, while colored women do not know scarcely anything. They go out washing, which is about as high as a colored woman gets, and their men go about idle, strutting up and down; and when the women come home, they ask for their money and take it all, and then scold because there is no food. I want you to consider on that, chil'n I call you chil'n; you are somebody's chil'n and I am old enough to be mother of all that is here. I want women to have their rights. In the courts women have no right, no voice; nobody speaks for them. I wish woman to have her voice there among the pettifoggers. If it is not a fit place for women, it is unfit for men to be there. I am above eighty years old; it is about time for me to be going. I have been forty years a slave and forty years free, and would be here forty years more to have equal rights for all. I suppose I am kept here because something remains for me to do, I suppose I am yet to help to break the chain. I have done a great deal of work; as much as a man, but did not get so much pay. I used to work in the field and bind grain, keeping up with the cradler; but men doing no more, got twice as much pay; so with the German women. They work in the field and do as much work, but do not got the pay. We do as much, we eat as much, we want as much. I suppose I am about the only colored woman that goes about to speak for the rights of the colored women. I want to keep the thing stirring, now that the ice is cracked. What we want is a little money.

You men know that you get as much again as women when you write, or for what you do. When we get our rights we shall not have to come to you for money, for then we shall have money enough in our own pockets; and may be you will ask us for money. But help us now until we get it. It is a good consolation to know that when we have got this battle once fought we shall not be coming to you any more. You have been having our rights so long, that you think, like a slave-holder, that you own us. I know that it is hard for one who has held the reins for so long to give up; it cuts like a knife. It will feel all the better when it closes up again. I have been in Washington about three years, seeing about these colored people. Now colored men have the right to vote. There ought to be equal rights now more than ever, since colored people have got their freedom. I am going to talk several times while I am here; so now I will do a little singing. I have not heard any singing since I came here.

(Accordingly, suiting the action to the word, Sojourner sang "We Are Going Home.")

There, children, said she, after singing, we shall rest from all our labors; first do all we have to do here. There I am determined to go, not to stop short of that beautiful place, and I do not mean to stop till I get there, and meet you there too.

Ain't I a Woman

Women's Rights Convention, May 29, 1851, Akron, Ohio

May I say a few words? Receiving an affirmative answer, she proceeded; I want to say a few words about this matter. I am a woman's rights. I have as much muscle as any man, and can do as much work as any man. I have plowed and reaped and husked and chopped and mowed, and can any man do more than that? I have heard much about the sexes being equal; I can carry as much as any man, and can eat as much too, if I can get it. I am strong as any man that is now.

As for intellect, all I can say is, if woman have a pint and man a quart—why can't she have her little pint full? You need not be afraid to give us our rights for fear we will take too much—for we won't take more than our pint'll hold.

The poor men seem to be all in confusion and don't know what to do. Why children, if you have woman's rights give it to her and you will feel better. You will have your own rights, and they won't be so much trouble.

I can't read, but I can hear. I have heard the Bible and have learned that Eve caused man to sin. Well if woman upset the world, do give her a chance to set it right side up again. The lady has spoken about Jesus, how he never spurned woman from him, and she was right. When Lazarus died, Mary and Martha came to him with faith and love and besought him to raise their brother. And Jesus wept—and Lazarus came forth. And how came Jesus into the world? Through God who created him and woman who bore him. Man, where is your part?

But the women are coming up blessed be God and a few of the men are coming up with them. But man is in a tight place, the poor slave is on him, woman is coming on him, and he is surely between a hawk and a buzzard.

Suppose I Am About the Only Colored Woman to Speak for the Rights of Colored Women

Fourth National Woman's Rights Convention,
September 7, 1853, New York, New York

Is it not good for me to come and draw forth a spirit, to see what kind of spirit people are of? I see that some of you have got the spirit of a goose, and some have got the spirit of a snake. I feel at home here. I come to you, citizens of New York, as I suppose you ought to be. I am citizen of the state of New York; I was born in it, and I was a slave in the state of New York; and now I am a good citizen of this State. I was born here, and I can tell you I feel at home here. I've been lookin' round and watchin' things, and I know a little mite 'bout Woman's Rights, too. I come forth to speak 'bout Woman's Rights, and want to throw in my little mite, to keep the scales a-movin'. I know that it feels a kind o' hissin' and ticklin' like to see a colored woman get up again; but we have been long enough trodden now; we will come up again, and now I am here.

I was a-thinkin', when I see woman contendin' for their rights, I was a-thinkin' what a difference there is now, and what there was in old times. I have only a few minutes to speak; but in the old times the kings of the earth would hear a woman. There was a king in the Scriptures; and then it was the kings of the earth would kill a woman if she come into presence; but Queen Esther come forth, for she was oppressed, and felt there was a great wrong, and she said I will die or I will bring my complaint before the king. Should the king of the United States be greater, or more crueler, or more harder? But the King, he raised up his scepter and said: "Thy request shall be granted unto thee—to the half of my kingdom will I grant it to thee!" Then he said he would hang Haman on the gallows he had made up high. But that is not what women come forward to contend. The women want their rights as Esther. She only wanted to explain her rights. And he was so liberal that he said, "the half of my kingdom shall be granted to thee," and he did not wait for her to ask, he was so liberal with her.

Now, women do not ask half a kingdom, but their rights, and they don't get 'em. When she comes to demand 'em, don't you hear how sons hiss their mothers like snakes, because they ask for their rights; and can they ask for anything less? The king ordered Haman to be hung on the gallows which he prepared to hang others; but I do not want any man to be killers, but I am sorry to see them so short-minded. But we'll have our rights; see if we don't; and you can't stop us from them; see if you can. You may hiss as much as you like, but it is comin'. Women don't get half as much rights as they ought to; we want more, and we, we will have it. Jesus says: "What I say to one, I say to all-watch!" I'm a-watchin'. God says: "Honor your father and your mother." Sons and daughter ought to behave themselves before their mothers, but they do not. I can see them a-laughin' and pointin' at their mothers up here on the stage. They hiss when an aged woman comes forth. If they'd been brought up proper they'd have known better than hissing like snakes and geese. I'm 'round watchin' these things, and I wanted to come up and say these few things to you, and I'm glad of the hearin' you give me. I wanted to tell you a mite about Woman's Rights, and so I came out and said so. I am sittin' among you to watch; and every once and awhile I will come out and tell you what time of night it is.

2

Harriet Tubman

1822–1913

Known as the "Moses of her people," Harriet Tubman was enslaved and escaped and helped others gain their freedom as a "conductor" of the Underground Railroad. Tubman also served as a scout, spy, guerrilla soldier, and nurse for the Union army during the Civil War. She is considered the first African American woman to serve in the military.

Liberty or Death

From the book *Harriet: The Moses of Her People*
by Sarah H. Bradford

"For," said she, "I had reasoned dis out in my mind; there was one of two things I had a *right* to, liberty, or death; if I could not have one, I would have de oder; for no man should take me alive; I should fight for my liberty as long as my strength lasted, and when de time came for me to go, de Lord would let dem take me."

And so without money, and without friends, she started on through unknown regions; walking by night, hiding by day, but always conscious of an invisible pillar of cloud by day, and of fire by night, under the guidance of which she journeyed or rested. Without knowing whom to trust, or how near the pursuers might be, she carefully felt her way, and by her native cunning, or by God given wisdom, she managed to apply to the right people for food, and sometimes for shelter; though often her bed was only the cold ground, and her watcher the stars of night.

After many long and weary days of travel, she found that she had passed the magic line, which then divided the land of bondage from the land of freedom. But where were the lovely white ladies whom in her visions she had seen, who, with arms outstretched, welcomed her to their hearts and homes. All these visions proved deceitful: she was more alone than ever; but she had crossed the line; no one could take her now, and she would never call any man "Master" more.

"I looked at my hands," she said, "to see if I was de same person now I was free. Dere was such a glory ober everything, de sun came like fold trou de trees, and ober de fields, and I felt like I was in heaven." But then came the bitter drop in the cup of joy. She was alone, and her kindred were in slavery, and not one of them had the courage to dare what she had dared. Unless she made the effort to liberate them she would never see them more, or even know of their fate.

"I knew of a man, she said, "who was sent to the State Prison for twenty-five years. All these years he was always thinking of him home, and counting by years, months, and days, the time till he should be free, and see his family and friends once more. The years roll on, the time of imprisonment is over, the man is free. He leaves the prison gates, he makes his way to his old home, but his old home is not there. The house in which he had dwelt in his childhood had been torn down, and a new one had been put up in its place; his family were gone, their very name was forgotten, there was no one to take him by the hand to welcome him back to life."

"So it was wid me," said Harriet, "I had crossed de line of which I had so long been dreaming. I was free; but dere was no one to welcome me to de land of freedom, I was a stranger in a strange land, and my home after all was down in de old cabin quarter, wid de old folks, and my brudders and sisters. But to dis solemn resolution I came; I was free, and dey should be free also; I would make a home for dem in de North, and de Lord helping me, I would bring dem all here. Oh how I prayed den, lying all alone on de cold, damp ground; "Oh, dear Lord," I said, "I haint got no friend but *you.* Come to my help, Lord, for I'm in trouble!"

3

Mary Ann Shadd Cary

1823-1893

Mary Ann Shadd Cary, born in Wilmington, Delaware, the eldest of thirteen children of free Black American parents, became a role model for women in education and law. After receiving an education from Pennsylvania Quakers, Cary devoted the first part of her life to advocating for abolition, working with fugitive slaves, and becoming the first Black woman in North America to edit a weekly newspaper—the *Provincial Freeman*—which served displaced African Americans living in Canada.

Break Every Yoke and Let the Oppressed Go Free

Appearing in the *Provincial Freeman*, April 6, 1858

Cary opened a debate on the merits of emigration to Canada by free people of color.

1st business of life—[to] love the Lord our God with heart and soul, and our neighbor as our self.

[We] must then manifest [love] to God by obedience to his will—we must be cheerful workers, in his cause at all times—on the Sabbath and other days[.]

The more [readiness] we Evince the more we manifest our love, and as our field is [directly] among those of his creatures made in his own image in acting as themself who is no respecter of persons we must have failed in our duty until we become decided to waive all prejudices of education[,] birth nation or training and make the test of our obedience God's [equal] command to love the neighbor as ourselves.

These two great commandments, and upon which [rest] all the [Love] and the prophets, cannot be narrowed down to suit us [but] we must go [up] and conform [to] them. They proscribe neither nation nor sex—our neighbor may be Either the oriental heathen the degraded Europe and or the Enslaved colored American. Neither must we prefer sex the Slave mother as well as the Slave father. The oppress, or nominally free woman of every nation or clime in whose Soul is as Evident by the image of God as in her more fortunate contemporary of the male sex has a claim upon us by virtue of that irrevocable command Equally as urgent. We cannot successfully Evade duty because the Suffering fellow woman be is only a woman! She too is a neighbor. The good Samaritan of this generation must not take for their Exemplars the priest and the Levite when a fellow wom[an] is among thieves—neither will they find their Excuse in the custom as barbarous and anti-christian as any promulgated by pious Brahmin that [*word crossed out*] they may be only females. The spirit of true philanthropy knows no sex. The true christian will not seek to Exhume from the grave of the past [*word crossed out*] its half-developed customs and insist upon them as a substitute for the plain teachings of Jesus Christ, and the Evident deductions of a more Enlightened humanity.

There is too a fitness of time for any work for the benefit of God's human creatures. We are told to keep Holy the Sabbath day. In what manner? Not by following simply the injunctions of those who bind heavy burdens, to say nothing about the same but as a man is better than a sheep but combining with God's worship the most active vigilance for the resurector from degradation violence and sin his creatures. In these cases particularly was the Sabbath made for man and woman if you please as there may be those who will not accept the term man in a generic sense. Christ has told us as it is lawful to lift a sheep out of the ditch on the Sabbath day, i[f] a man is much better than a sheep.

Those with whom I am identified, namely the colored people of this country–and the women of the land are in the pit figurat[ively] speaking are cast out. These were Gods requirements during the Prophecy of Isaiah and they are in full force today. God is the same yesterday today and forever. And upon this nation and to this people they come with all their significance within your grasp are three or four millions in chains in your southern territory and among and around about you are half a million allied to them by blood and to you by blood as were the Hebrew servants who realize the intensity of your hatred and oppression. You are the government what it does to [th] you Enslaves the poor whites The free colored people The Example of slave holders to access all.

What we aim to do is to put away this Evil from among you and thereby pay a debt you now owe to humanity and to God and so turn from their channel the bitter waters of a moral servitude that is about overwhelming yourselves.

I speak plainly because of a common origin and because were it not for the monster slavery we would have a common destiny here—in the land of our birth. And because the policy of the American government so singularly set aside allows to all free speech and free thought: As the law of God must be to us the higher law in spite of powers principalities selfish priests or selfish people to whom the minister it is important the [that?] we assert boldly that no where does God look upon this the chief crimes with the least degree of allowance nor are we justified in asserting that he will tolerate those who in any wise support or sustain it.

Slavery American slavery will not bear moral tests. It is in Exists by striking down all the moral safeguards to society by—it is not then a moral institution. You are called upon as a man to deny and disobey the most noble impulses of manhood to aid a brother in distress—to refuse to strike from the limbs of those not bound for any crime the fetters by which his Escape is obstructed. The milk of human kindness must be transformed into the bitter waters of hatred—you must return to his master he that hath Escaped, no matter how Every principle of manly independence revolts at the same. This feeling Extends to Every one allied by blood to the slave. And while we have in the North those who stand as guards to the institution they must also volunteer as [s]hippers away of the nominally free. You must drive from this home by a hartless ostracism to the heathen shores when they fasted, bowed themselves, and spread sack cloth and ashes under them. Made long prayers (&c.] that they might be seen of men, but Isaiah told them God would not accept them. They must repent of their sins—put away iniquity from among them and then should their light shine forth.

But we are or may be told that slavery is only an Evil not a sin, and that too by those who say it was allowed among the Jews and therefore ought to be Endured. Isaiah sets that matter to rest he shows that it is a sin handling it less delicately than many prophets in this generation. These are the sins that we are to spare not the sin of Enslaving men—of keeping back the hire of the laborer. You are to loose the bands of wickedness, to undo the heavy burdens to break Every yoke and to let the oppressed go free. To deal out bread to the hungry and to bring the poor [*word missing*] speaking. Their cry has long been ascending to the Lord who then will assume the responsibility of prescribing times and seasons and [*word crossed out*] for the pleading of their cause—of and righteous cause—and who shall overrule the voice of woman? Emphatically the greatest sufferer from chattel slavery or political proscription on this God's footstool? Nay we have Christ's Example who held the sexes indiscriminately thereby implying an Equal inheritance—who rebuffed the worldling Martha and approved innovator Mary. [The Him] who respected not persons [*two words crossed out*] but who imposes Christian duties alike upon all sexes, and who in his wise providence metes out his retribution alike upon all.

No friends we suffer the oppressors of the age to lead us astray; instead of going to the source of truth for guidance we let the adversary guide us as to what is our duty and Gods word. The Jews thought to that they were doing [H]is requirements when they did only that which was but a small sacrifice.

4

Frances Ellen Watkins Harper

1825–1911

Frances Ellen Watkins Harper was a lecturer, author, poet, and civil rights activist. She was said to be the first African American woman to publish a short story. An abolitionist and suffragist, she co-founded the National Association of Colored Women's Clubs.

We Are All Bound Up Together

Eleventh National Woman's Rights Convention, May 1, 1866, New York, New York

---

In May 1866, Frances Ellen Watkins Harper, a leading poet, lecturer, and civil right activist, addressed the Eleventh National Woman's Rights Convention in New York, joining Elizabeth Cady Stanton, Susan B. Anthony, and Lucretia Mott, who were among the featured speakers. Her address appears below.

I feel I am something of a novice upon this platform. Born of a race whose inheritance has been outrage and wrong, most of my life had been spent in battling against those wrongs. But I did not feel as keenly as others, that I had these rights, in common with other women, which are now demanded. About two years ago, I stood within the shadows of my home. A great sorrow had fallen upon my life. My husband had died suddenly, leaving me a widow, with four children, one my own, and the others step-children. I tried to keep my children together. But my husband died in debt; and before he had been in his grave three months, the administrator had swept the very milk crocks and wash tubs from my hands. I was a farmer's wife and made butter for the Columbus market; but what could I do, when they had swept all away? They left me one thing and that was a looking glass! Had I died instead of my husband, how different would have been the result! By this time he would have had another wife, it is likely; and no administrator would have gone into his house, broken up his home, and sold his bed, and taken away his means of support.

I took my children in my arms, and went out to seek my living. While I was gone; a neighbor to whom I had once lent five dollars, went before a magistrate and swore that he believed I was a non resident, and laid an attachment on my very bed. And I went back to Ohio with my orphan children in my arms, without a single feather bed in this wide world, that was not in the custody of the law. I say, then, that justice is not fulfilled so long as woman is unequal before the law.

We are all bound up together in one great bundle of humanity, and society cannot trample on the weakest and feeblest of its members without receiving the curse in its own soul. You tried that in the case of the negro. You pressed him down for two centuries; and in so doing you crippled the moral strength and paralyzed the spiritual energies of the white men of the country. When the hands of the black were fettered, white men were deprived of the liberty of speech and the freedom of the press. Society cannot afford to neglect the enlightenment of any class of its members. At the South, the legislation of the country was in behalf of the rich slaveholders, while the poor white man was neglected. What is the consequence to day? From that very class of neglected poor white men, comes the man who stands to day, with his hand upon the helm of the nation. He fails to catch the watchword of the hour, and throws himself, the incarnation of meanness, across the pathway of the nation. My objection to Andrew Johnson is not that he has been a poor white man; my objection is that he keeps "poor whites" all the way through. (Applause.) That is the trouble with him.

This grand and glorious revolution which has commenced, will fail to reach its climax of success, until throughout the length and brea[d]th of the American Republic, the nation shall be so color-blind, as to know no man by the color of his skin or the curl of his hair. It will then have no privileged class, trampling upon outraging the unprivileged classes, but will be then one great privileged nation, whose privilege will be to produce the loftiest manhood and womanhood that humanity can attain.

I do not believe that giving the woman the ballot is immediately going to cure all the ills of life. I do not believe that white women are dew-drops just exhaled from the skies. I think that like men they may be divided into three classes, the good, the bad, and the indifferent. The good would vote according to their convictions and principles; the bad, as dictated by preju[d]ice or malice; and the indifferent will vote on the strongest side of the question, with the winning party.

You white women speak here of rights. I speak of wrongs. I, as a colored woman, have had in this country an education which has made me feel as if I were in the situation of Ishmael, my hand against every man, and every man's hand against me. Let me go to-morrow morning and take my seat in one of your street cars—I do not know that they will do it in New York, but they will in Philadelphia—and the conductor will put up his hand and stop the car rather than let me ride.

A Lady—They will not do that here.

Mrs. Harper—They do in Philadelphia. Going from Washington to Baltimore this Spring, they put me in the smoking car. (Loud Voices—"Shame.") Aye, in the capital of the nation, where the black man consecrated himself to the nation's defence, faithful when the white man was faithless, they put me in the smoking car! They did it once; but the next time they tried it, they failed; for I would not go in. I felt the fight in me; but I don't want to have to fight all the time. To-day I am puzzled where to make my home. I would like to make it in Philadelphia, near my own friends and relations. But if I want to ride in the streets of Philadelphia, they send me to ride on the platform with the driver. (Cries of "Shame.") Have women nothing to do with this? Not long since, a colored woman took her seat in an Eleventh Street car in Philadelphia, and the conductor stopped the car, and told the rest of the passengers to get out, and left the car with her in it alone, when they took it back to the station. One day I took my seat in a car, and the conductor came to me and told me to take another seat. I just screamed "murder." The man said if I was black I ought to behave myself. I knew that if he was white he was not behaving himself. Are there no wrongs to be righted?

In advocating the cause of the colored man, since the Dred Scott decision, I have sometimes said I thought the nation had touched bottom. But let me tell you there is a depth of infamy lower than that. It is when the nation, standing upon the threshold of a great peril, reached out its hands to a feebler race, and asked that race to help it, and when the peril was over, said, You are good enough for soldiers, but not good enough for citizens. When Judge Taney said that the men of my race had no rights which the white man was bound to respect, he had not seen the bones of the black man bleaching outside of Richmond. He had not seen the thinned ranks and the thickened graves of the Louisiana Second, a regiment which went into battle nine hundred strong, and came out with three hundred. He had not stood at Olustee and seen defeat and disaster crushing down the pride of our banner, until words was brought to Col. Hallowell, "The day is lost; go in and save it;" and black men stood in the gap, beat back the enemy, and saved your army. (Applause.)

We have a woman in our country who has received the name of "Moses," not by lying about it, but by acting out (applause)—a woman who has gone down into the Egypt of slavery an brought out hundreds of our people into liberty. The last time I saw that woman, her hands were swollen. That woman who had led one of Montgomery's most successful expeditions, who was brave enough and secretive enough to act as a scout for the American army, had her hands all swollen from a conflict with a brutal conductor, who undertook to eject her from her place. That woman, whose courage and bravery won a recognition from our army and from every black man in the land, is excluded from every thoroughfare of travel. Talk of giving women the ballot-box? Go on. It is a normal school, and the white women of this country need it. While there exists this brutal element in society which tramples upon the feeble and treads down the weak, I tell you that if there is any class of people who need to be lifted out of their airy nothings and selfishness, it is the white women of America. (Applause.)

Woman's Political Future

Address before the World's Congress of Representative Women at the World's Columbian Exposition, May 20, 1893, Chicago, Illinois

---

If before sin had cast its deepest shadows or sorrow had distilled its bitterest tears, it was true that it was not good for man to be alone, it is no less true, since the shadows have deepened and life's sorrows have increased, that the world has need of all the spiritual aid that woman can give for the social advancement and moral development of the human race. The tendency of the present age, with its restlessness, religious upheavals, failures, blunders, and crimes, is toward broader freedom, an increase of knowledge, the emancipation of thought, and a recognition of the brotherhood of man; in this movement woman, as the companion of man, must be a sharer. So close is the bond between man and woman that you can not raise one without lifting the other. The world can not move without woman's sharing in the movement, and to help give a right impetus to that movement is woman's highest privilege.

If the fifteenth century discovered America to the Old World, the nineteenth is discovering woman to herself. Little did Columbus imagine, when the New World broke upon his vision like a lovely gem in the coronet of the universe, the glorious possibilities of a land where the sun should be our engraver, the winged lightning our messenger, and steam our beast of burden. But as mind is more than matter, and the highest ideal always the true real, so to woman comes the opportunity to strive for richer and grander discoveries than ever gladdened the eye of the Genoese mariner.

Not the opportunity of discovering new worlds, but that of filling this old world with fairer and higher aims than the greed of gold and the lust of power, is hers. Through weary, wasting years men have destroyed, dashed in pieces, and overthrown, but to-day we stand on the threshold of woman's era, and woman's work is grandly constructive. In her hand are possibilities whose use or abuse must tell upon the political life of the nation, and send their influence for good or evil across the track of unborn ages.

As the saffron tints and crimson flushes of morn herald the coming day, so the social and political advancement which woman has already gained bears the promise of the rising of the full-orbed sun of emancipation. The result will be not to make home less happy, but society more holy; yet I do not think the mere extension of the ballot a panacea for all the ills of our national life. What we need to-day is not simply more voters, but better voters. To-day there are red-handed men in our republic, who walk unwhipped of justice, who richly deserve to exchange the ballot of the freeman for the wristlets of the felon; brutal and cowardly men, who torture, burn, and lynch their fellow-men, men whose defenselessness should be their best defense and their weakness an ensign of protection. More than the changing of institutions we need the development of a national conscience, and the upbuilding of national character. Men may boast of the aristocracy of blood, may glory in the aristocracy of talent, and be proud of the aristocracy of wealth, but there is one aristocracy which must ever outrank them all, and that is the aristocracy of character; and it is the women of a country who help to mold its character, and to influence if not determine its destiny; and in the political future of our nation woman will not have done what she could if she does not endeavor to have our republic stand foremost among the nations of the earth, wearing sobriety as a crown and righteousness as a garment and a girdle. In coming into her political estate woman will find a mass of illiteracy to be dispelled. If knowledge is power, ignorance is also power. The power that educates wickedness may manipulate and dash against the pillars of any state when they are undermined and honey-combed by injustice.

I envy neither the heart nor the head of any legislator who has been born to an inheritance of privileges, who has behind him ages of education, dominion, civilization, and Christianity, if he stands opposed to the passage of a national education bill, whose purpose is to secure education to the children of those who were born under the shadow of institutions which made it a crime to read.

To-day women hold in their hands influence and opportunity, and with these they have already opened doors which have been closed to others. By opening doors of labor woman has become a rival claimant for at least some of the wealth monopolized by her stronger brother. In the home she is the priestess, in society the queen, in literature she is a power, in legislative halls law-makers have responded to her appeals, and for her sake have humanized and liberalized their laws. The press has felt the impress of her hand. In the pews of the church she constitutes the majority; the pulpit has welcomed her, and in the school she has the blessed privilege of teaching children and youth. To her is apparently coming the added responsibility of political power; and what she now possesses should only be the means of preparing her to use the coming power for the glory of God and the good of mankind; for power without righteousness is one of the most dangerous forces in the world.

Political life in our country has plowed in muddy channels, and needs the infusion of clearer and cleaner waters. I am not sure that women are naturally so much better than men that they will clear the stream by the virtue of their womanhood; it is not through sex but through character that the best influence of women upon the life of the nation must be exerted.

I do not believe in unrestricted and universal suffrage for either men or women. I believe in moral and educational tests. I do not believe that the most ignorant and brutal man is better prepared to add value to the strength and durability of the government than the most cultured, upright, and intelligent woman. I do not think that willful ignorance should swamp earnest intelligence at the ballot-box, nor that educated wickedness, violence, and fraud should cancel the votes of honest men. The unsteady hands of a drunkard can not cast the ballot of a freeman. The hands of lynchers are too red with blood to determine the political character of the government for even four short years. The ballot in the hands of woman means power added to influence. How well she will use that power I can not foretell. Great evils stare us in the face that need to be throttled by the combined power of an upright manhood and an enlightened womanhood; and I know that no nation can gain its full measure of enlightenment and happiness if one-half of it is free and the other half is fettered. China compressed the feet of her women and thereby retarded the steps of her men. The elements of a nation's weakness must ever be found at the hearthstone.

More than the increase of wealth, the power of armies, and the strength of fleets is the need of good homes, of good fathers, and good mothers.

The life of a Roman citizen was in danger in ancient Palestine, and men had bound themselves with a vow that they would eat nothing until they had killed the Apostle Paul. Pagan Rome threw around that imperiled life a bulwark of living clay consisting of four hundred and seventy human hearts, and Paul was saved. Surely the life of the humblest American citizen should be as well protected in America as that of a Roman citizen was in heathen Rome. A wrong done to the weak should be an insult to the strong. Woman coming into her kingdom will find enthroned three great evils, for whose overthrow she should be as strong in a love of justice and humanity as the warrior is in his might. She will find intemperance sending its flood of shame, and death, and sorrow to the homes of men, a fretting leprosy in our politics, and a blighting curse in our social life; the social evil sending to our streets women whose laughter is sadder than their tears, who slide from the paths of sin and shame to the friendly shelter of the grave; and lawlessness enacting in our republic deeds over which angels might weep, if heaven knows sympathy.

How can any woman send petitions to Russia against the horrors of Siberian prisons if, ages after the Inquisition has ceased to devise its tortures, she has not done all she could by influence, tongue, and pen to keep men from making bonfires of the bodies of real or supposed criminals?

O women of America! into your hands God has pressed one of the sublimest opportunities that ever came into the hands of the women of any race or people. It is yours to create a healthy public sentiment; to demand justice, simple justice, as the right of every race; to brand with everlasting infamy the lawless and brutal cowardice that lynches, burns, and tortures your own countrymen.

To grapple with the evils which threaten to undermine the strength of the nation and to lay magazines of powder under the cribs of future generations is no child's play.

Let the hearts of the women of the world respond to the song of the herald angels of peace on earth and good will to men. Let them throb as one heart unified by the grand and holy purpose of uplifting the human race, and humanity will breathe freer, and the world grow brighter. With such a purpose Eden would spring up in our path, and Paradise be around our way.

5

Anna Julia Cooper

1858–1964

Born a slave, Anna Julia Cooper forged a life of stellar accomplishments. Co-founder of the Colored Women's League in 1892, she became a leader of human and civil rights for women and Black people, an educator, an author, and a scholar—one of the first Black women to earn a doctorate, in 1925.

Women's Cause Is One and Universal

World's Congress of Representative Women, May 18, 1893, Chicago, Illinois

On May 18, 1893, Anna Julia Cooper delivered an address at the World's Congress of Representative Women, then meeting in Chicago. Cooper's speech to this predominately white audience described the progress of African American women since slavery.

The higher fruits of civilization cannot be extemporized, neither can they be developed normally, in the brief space of thirty years. It requires the long and painful growth of generations. Yet all through the darkest period of the colored women's oppression in this country her yet unwritten history is full of heroic struggle, a struggle against fearful and overwhelming odds, that often ended in a horrible death, to maintain and protect that which woman holds dearer than life. The painful, patient, and silent toil of mothers to gain a free simple title to the bodies of their daughters, the despairing fight, as of an entrapped tigress, to keep hallowed their own persons, would furnish material for epics. That more went down under the flood than stemmed the current is not extraordinary.

The majority of our women are not heroines but I do not know that a majority of any race of women are heroines. It is enough for me to know that while in the eyes of the highest tribunal in America she was deemed no more than a chattel, an irresponsible thing, a dull block, to be drawn hither or thither at the volition of an owner, the Afro American woman maintained ideals of womanhood unshamed by any ever conceived. Resting or fermenting in untutored minds, such ideals could not claim a hearing at the bar of the nation. The white woman could least plead for her own emancipation; the black woman, doubly enslaved, could but suffer and struggle and be silent. I speak for the colored women of the South, because it is there that the millions of blacks in this country have watered the soil with blood and tears, and it is there too that the colored woman of America has made her characteristic history, and there her destiny evolving. Since emancipation the movement has been at times confused and stormy, so that we could not always tell whether we were going forward or groping in a circle. We hardly knew what we ought to emphasize, whether education or wealth, or civil freedom and recognition. We were utterly destitute. Possessing no homes nor the knowledge of how to make them, no money nor the habit of acquiring it, no education, no political status, no influence, what could we do? But as Frederick Douglass had said in darker days than those, "One with God is a majority," and our ignorance had hedged us in from the fine spun theories of agnostics. We had remaining at least a simple faith that a just God is on the throne of the universe, and that somehow—we could not see, nor did we bother our heads to try to tell how—he would in his own good time make all right that seemed most wrong.

Schools were established, not merely public day schools, but home training and industrial schools, at Hampton, at Fisk, Atlanta, Raleigh, and other stations, and later, through the energy of the colored people themselves, such schools as the Wilberforce, the Livingstone, the Allen, and the Paul Quinn were opened. These schools were almost without exception co-educational. Funds were too limited to be divided on sex lines, even had it been ideally desirable; but our girls as well as our boys flocked in and battled for an education. Not even then was that patient, untrumpeted heroine, the slave-mother, released from self-sacrifice, and many an unbuttered crust was eaten in silent content that she might eke out enough from her poverty to send her young folks off to school. She "never had the chance," she would tell you, with tears on her withered cheek, so she wanted them to get all they could. The work in these schools, and in such as these, has been like the little leaven hid in the measure of meal, permeating life throughout the length and breadth of the Southland, lifting up ideals of home and of womanhood; diffusing a contagious longing for higher living and purer thinking, inspiring woman herself with a new sense of her dignity in the eternal purposes of nature. Today there are twenty-five thousand five hundred and thirty colored schools in the United States with one million three hundred and fifty-three thousand three hundred and fifty-two pupils of both sexes. This is not quite the thirtieth year since their emancipation, and the color people hold in landed property for churches and schools twenty-five million dollars. Two and one half million colored children have learned to read and write, and twenty-two thousand nine hundred and fifty-six colored men and women (mostly women) are teaching in these schools. According to Doctor Rankin, President of Howard University, there are two hundred and forty seven colored students (a large percentage of whom are women) now preparing themselves in the universities of Europe. Of other colleges which give the B.A. course to women, and are broad enough not to erect barriers against colored applicants, Oberlin, the first to open its doors to both woman and the negro, has given classical degrees to six colored women, one of whom, the first and most eminent, Fannie Jackson Coppin, we shall listen to tonight.

Ann Arbor and Wellesley have each graduated three of our women; Cornell University one, who is now professor of sciences in a Washington high school. A former pupil of my own from the Washington High School who was snubbed by Vassar, has since carried off honors in a competitive examination in Chicago University. The medical and law colleges of country are likewise bombarded by colored women, and every year some sister of the darker race claims their professional award of "well done." Eminent in their profession are Doctor Dillon and Doctor James, and there sailed to Africa last month a demure little brown woman who had just outstripped a whole class of men in a medical college in Tennessee.

In organized efforts for self-help and benevolence also our women been active. The Colored Women's League, of which I am at present corresponding secretary, has active, energetic branches in the South and West. The branch in Kansas City, with a membership of upward of one hundred and fifty, already has begun under their vigorous president, Mrs. Yates, the erection of a building for friendless girls. Mrs. Coppin will, I hope, herself tell you something of her own magnificent creation of an industrial society in Philadelphia. The women of the Washington branch of the league have subscribed to a fund of about five thousand dollars to erect a woman's building for educational and industrial work, which is also to serve as headquarters for gathering and disseminating general information relating to the efforts of our women. This is just a glimpse of what we are doing.

Now, I think if I could crystallize the sentiment of my constituency, and deliver it as a message to this congress of women, it would be something like this: Let woman's claim be as broad in the concrete as in the abstract. We take our stand on the solidarity of humanity, the oneness of life, and the unnaturalness and injustice of all special favoritisms, whether of sex, race, country, or condition. If one link of the chain be broken, the chain is broken. A bridge is no stronger than its weakest part, and a cause is not worthier than its weakest element. Least of all can woman's cause afford to decry the weak. We want, then, as toilers for the universal triumph of justice and human rights, to go to our homes from this Congress, demanding an entrance not through a gateway for ourselves, our race, our sex, or our sect, but a grand highway for humanity. The colored woman feels that woman's cause is one and universal; and that not till the image of God, whether in parian or ebony, is sacred and inviolable; not till race, color, sex, and condition are seen as the accidents, and not the substance of life; not till the universal title of humanity to life, liberty, and the pursuit of happiness is conceded to be inalienable to all; not till then is woman's lesson taught and woman's cause won—not the white woman's, nor the black woman's, not the red woman's, but the cause of every man and of every woman who has writhed silently under a mighty wrong. Woman's wrongs are thus indissolubly linked with undefended woe, and the acquirement of her "rights" will mean the final triumph of all right over might, the supremacy of the moral forces of reason, and justice, and love in the government of the nations of earth.

6

Ida B. Wells-Barnett

1862–1931

Ida B. Wells-Barnett, born in slavery, went on to forge a storied life as an abolitionist and steadfast fighter for women's equality and racial justice. As a journalist, she was among the first to cover lynchings and other atrocities, putting her life in danger to expose the racial violence that was sweeping across the nation in the late nineteenth century. She went on to lecture around the world, holding America accountable for its entrenched racism and sexism.

Lynch Law in America

1900, Chicago, Illinois

Our country's national crime is lynching. It is not the creature of an hour, the sudden outburst of uncontrolled fury, or the unspeakable brutality of an insane mob. It represents the cool, calculating deliberation of intelligent people who openly avow that there is an "unwritten law" that justifies them in putting human beings to death without complaint under oath, without trial by jury, without opportunity to make defense, and without right of appeal. The "unwritten law" first found excuse with the rough, rugged, and determined man who left the civilized centers of eastern States to seek for quick returns in the gold fields of the far West. Following in uncertain pursuit of continually eluding fortune, they dared the savagery of the Indians, the hardships of mountain travel, and the constant terror of border State outlaws. Naturally, they felt slight toleration for traitors in their own ranks. It was enough to fight the enemies from without; woe to the foe within! Far removed from and entirely without protection of the courts of civilized life, these fortune-seekers made laws to meet their varying emergencies. The thief who stole a horse, the bully who "jumped" a claim, was a common enemy. If caught he was promptly tried, and if found guilty was hanged to the tree under which the court convened.

Those were busy days of busy men. They had no time to give the prisoner a bill of exception or stay of execution. The only way a man had to secure a stay of execution was to behave himself. Judge Lynch was original in methods but exceedingly effective in procedure. He made the charge, impaneled the jurors, and directed the execution. When the court adjourned, the prisoner was dead. Thus lynch law held sway in the far West until civilization spread into the Territories and the orderly processes of law took its place. The emergency no longer existing, lynching gradually disappeared from the West.

But the spirit of mob procedure seemed to have fastened itself upon the lawless classes, and the grim process that at first was invoked to declare justice was made the excuse to wreak vengeance and cover crime. It next appeared in the South, where centuries of Anglo-Saxon civilization had made effective all the safeguards of court procedure. No emergency called for lynch law. It asserted its sway in defiance of law and in favor of anarchy. There it has flourished ever since, marking the thirty years of its existence with the inhuman butchery of more than ten thousand men, women, and children by shooting, drowning, hanging, and burning them alive. Not only this, but so potent is the force of example that the lynching mania has spread throughout the North and middle West. It is now no uncommon thing to read of lynchings north of Mason and Dixon's line, and those most responsible for this fashion gleefully point to these instances and assert that the North is no better than the South.

This is the work of the "unwritten law" about which so much is said, and in whose behest butchery is made a pastime and national savagery condoned. The first statute of this "unwritten law" was written in the blood of thousands of brave men who thought that a government that was good enough to create a citizenship was strong enough to protect it. Under the authority of a national law that gave every citizen the right to vote, the newly-made citizens chose to exercise their suffrage. But the reign of the national law was short-lived and illusionary. Hardly had the sentences dried upon the statute-books before one Southern State after another raised the cry against "negro domination" and proclaimed there was an "unwritten law" that justified any means to resist it.

The method then inaugurated was the outrages by the "red-shirt" bands of Louisiana, South Carolina, and other Southern States, which were succeeded by the Ku-Klux Klans. These advocates of the "unwritten law" boldly avowed their purpose to intimidate, suppress, and nullify the negro's right to vote. In support of its plans the Ku-Klux Klans, the "red-shirt" and similar organizations proceeded to beat, exile, and kill negroes until the purpose of their organization was accomplished and the supremacy of the "unwritten law" was effected. Thus lynchings began in the South, rapidly spreading into the various States until the national law was nullified and the reign of the "unwritten law" was supreme. Men were taken from their homes by "red-shirt" bands and stripped, beaten, and exiled; others were assassinated when their political prominence made them obnoxious to their political opponents; while the Ku-Klux barbarism of election days, reveling in the butchery of thousands of colored voters, furnished records in Congressional investigations that are a disgrace to civilization.

The alleged menace of universal suffrage having been avoided by the absolute suppression of the negro vote, the spirit of mob murder should have been satisfied and the butchery of negroes should have ceased. But men, women, and children were the victims of murder by individuals and murder by mobs, just as they had been when killed at the demands of the "unwritten law" to prevent "negro domination." Negroes were killed for disputing over terms of contracts with their employers. If a few barns were burned some colored man was killed to stop it. If a colored man resented the imposition of a white man and the two came to blows, the colored man had to die, either at the hands of the white man then and there or later at the hands of a mob that speedily gathered. If he showed a spirit of courageous manhood he was hanged for his pains, and the killing was justified by the declaration that he was a "saucy nigger." Colored women have been murdered because they refused to tell the mobs where relatives could be found for "lynching bees." Boys of fourteen years have been lynched by white representatives of American civilization. In fact, for all kinds of offenses—and, for no offenses—from murders to misdemeanors, men and women are put to death without judge or jury; so that, although the political excuse was no longer necessary, the wholesale murder of human beings went on just the same. A new name was given to the killings and a new excuse was invented for so doing.

Again, the aid of the "unwritten law" is invoked, and again it comes to the rescue. During the last ten years a new statute has been added to the "unwritten law." This statute proclaims that for certain crimes or alleged crimes no negro shall be allowed a trial; that no white woman shall be compelled to charge an assault under oath or to submit any such charge to the investigation of a court of law. The result is that many men have been put to death whose innocence was afterward established; and to-day, under this reign of the "unwritten law," no colored man, no matter what his reputation, is safe from lynching if a white woman, no matter what her standing or motive, cares to charge him with insult or assault.

It is considered a sufficient excuse and reasonable justification to put a prisoner to death under this "unwritten law" for the frequently repeated charge that these lynching horrors are necessary to prevent crimes against women. The sentiment of the country has been appealed to, in describing the isolated condition of white families in thickly populated negro districts; and the charge is made that these homes are in as great danger as if they were surrounded by wild beasts. And the world has accepted this theory without let or hindrance. In many cases there has been open expression that the fate meted out to the victim was only what he deserved. In many other instances there has been a silence that says more forcibly than words can proclaim it that it is right and proper that a human being should be seized by a mob and burned to death upon the unsworn and the uncorroborated charge of his accuser. No matter that our laws presume every man innocent until he is proved guilty; no matter that it leaves a certain class of individuals completely at the mercy of another class; no matter that it encourages those criminally disposed to blacken their faces and commit any crime in the calendar so long as they can throw suspicion on some negro, as is frequently done, and then lead a mob to take his life; no matter that mobs make a farce of the law and a mockery of justice; no matter that hundreds of boys are being hardened in crime and schooled in vice by the repetition of such scenes before their eyes—if a white woman declares herself insulted or assaulted, some life must pay the penalty, with all the horrors of the Spanish Inquisition and all the barbarism of the Middle Ages. The world looks on and says it is well.

Not only are two hundred men and women put to death annually, on the average, in this country by mobs, but these lives are taken with the greatest publicity. In many instances the leading citizens aid and abet by their presence when they do not participate, and the leading journals inflame the public mind to the lynching point with scare-head articles and offers of rewards. Whenever a burning is advertised to take place, the railroads run excursions, photographs are taken, and the same jubilee is indulged in that characterized the public hangings of one hundred years ago. There is, however, this difference: in those old days the multitude that stood by was permitted only to guy or jeer. The nineteenth century lynching mob cuts off ears, toes, and fingers, strips off flesh, and distributes portions of the body as souvenirs among the crowd. If the leaders of the mob are so minded, coal-oil is poured over the body and the victim is then roasted to death. This has been done in Texarkana and Paris, Tex., in Bardswell, Ky., and in Newman, Ga. In Paris the officers of the law delivered the prisoner to the mob. The mayor gave the school children a holiday and the railroads ran excursion trains so that the people might see a human being burned to death. In Texarkana, the year before, men and boys amused themselves by cutting off strips of flesh and thrusting knives into their helpless victim. At Newman, Ga., of the present year, the mob tried every conceivable torture to compel the victim to cry out and confess, before they set fire to the faggots that burned him. But their trouble was all in vain—he never uttered a cry, and they could not make him confess.

This condition of affairs were brutal enough and horrible enough if it were true that lynchings occurred only because of the commission of crimes against women—as is constantly declared by ministers, editors, lawyers, teachers, statesmen, and even by women themselves. It has been to the interest of those who did the lynching to blacken the good name of the helpless and defenseless victims of their hate. For this reason they publish at every possible opportunity this excuse for lynching, hoping thereby not only to palliate their own crime but at the same time to prove the negro a moral monster and unworthy of the respect and sympathy of the civilized world. But this alleged reason adds to the deliberate injustice of the mob's work. Instead of lynchings being caused by assaults upon women, the statistics show that not one-third of the victims of lynchings are even charged with such crimes. The Chicago Tribune, which publishes annually lynching statistics, is authority for the following:

In 1892, when lynching reached high-water mark, there were 241 persons lynched. The entire number is divided among the following States:

Alabama	Louisiana	Tennessee
Arkansas	Maryland	Texas
California	Mississippi	Virginia
Florida	Missouri	West Virginia
Georgia	Montana	Wyoming
Idaho	New York	Arizona Ter
Illinois	North Carolina	Oklahoma
Kansas	Ohio	
Kentucky	South Carolina	

Of this number, 160 were of negro descent. Four of them were lynched in New York, Ohio, and Kansas; the remainder were murdered in the South. Five of this number were females. The charges for which they were lynched cover a wide range. They are as follows:

Rape	Robbery	Insulting Women
Murder	Assault and Battery	Desperados
Rioting	Attempted Rape	Fraud
Race Prejudice	Suspected Robery	Attempted Murder
No Cause Given	Larceny	No offense stated, boy and girl
Incendiarism	Self-defense	

In the case of the boy and girl above referred to, their father, named Hastings, was accused of the murder of a white man. His fourteen-year-old daughter and sixteen-year-old son were hanged and their bodies filled with bullets; then the father was also lynched. This occurred in November 1892, at Jonesville, La.

Indeed, the record for the last twenty years shows exactly the same or a smaller proportion who have been charged with this horrible crime. Quite a number of the one-third alleged cases of assault that have been personally investigated by the writer have shown that there was no foundation in fact for the charges; yet the claim is not made that there were no real culprits among them. The negro has been too long associated with the white man not to have copied his vices as well as his virtues. But the negro resents and utterly repudiates the efforts to blacken his good name by asserting that assaults upon women are peculiar to his race. The negro has suffered far more from the commission of this crime against the women of his race by white men than the white race has ever suffered through his crimes. Very scant notice is taken of the matter when this is the condition of affairs. What becomes a crime deserving capital punishment when the tables are turned is a matter of small moment when the negro woman is the accusing party.

But since the world has accepted this false and unjust statement, and the burden of proof has been placed upon the negro to vindicate his race, he is taking steps to do so. The Anti-Lynching Bureau of the National Afro-American Council is arranging to have every lynching investigated and publish the facts to the world, as has been done in the case of Sam Hose, who was burned alive last April at Newman, Ga. The detective's report showed that Hose killed Cranford, his employer, in self-defense, and that, while a mob was organizing to hunt Hose to punish him for killing a white man, not till twenty-four hours after the murder was the charge of rape, embellished with psychological and physical impossibilities, circulated. That gave an impetus to the hunt, and the Atlanta Constitution's reward of $500 keyed the mob to the necessary burning and roasting pitch. Of five hundred newspaper clippings of that horrible affair, nine-tenths of them assumed Hose's guilt—simply because his murderers said so, and because it is the fashion to believe the negro peculiarly addicted to this species of crime. All the negro asks is justice—a fair and impartial trial in the courts of the country. That given, he will abide the result.

But this question affects the entire American nation, and from several points of view: First, on the ground of consistency. Our watchword has been "the land of the free and the home of the brave." Brave men do not gather by thousands to torture and murder a single individual, so gagged and bound he cannot make even feeble resistance or defense. Neither do brave men or women stand by and see such things done without compunction of conscience, nor read of them without protest. Our nation has been active and outspoken in its endeavors to right the wrongs of the Armenian Christian, the Russian Jew, the Irish Home Ruler, the native women of India, the Siberian exile, and the Cuban patriot. Surely it should be the nation's duty to correct its own evils!

Second, on the ground of economy. To those who fail to be convinced from any other point of view touching this momentous question, a consideration of the economic phase might not be amiss. It is generally known that mobs in Louisiana, Colorado, Wyoming, and other States have lynched subjects of other countries. When their different governments demanded satisfaction, our country was forced to confess her inability to protect said subjects in the several States because of our State-rights doctrines, or in turn demand punishment of the lynchers. This confession, while humiliating in the extreme, was not satisfactory; and, while the United States cannot protect, she can pay. This she has done, and it is certain will have to do again in the case of the recent lynching of Italians in Louisiana. The United States already has paid in indemnities for lynching nearly a half million dollars, as follows:

Paid China for Rock Springs (Wyo.) massacre	$147,748.74
Paid China for outrages on Pacific Coast	$276,619.75
Paid Italy for massacre of Italian prisoners at New Orleans	$24,330.90
Paid Italy for lynchings at Walsenburg, Col.	$10,000.00
Paid Great Britain for outrages on James Bain and Frederick Dawson	$2,800.00

Third, for the honor of Anglo-Saxon civilization. No scoffer at our boasted American civilization could say anything more harsh of it than does the American white man himself who says he is unable to protect the honor of his women without resort to such brutal, inhuman, and degrading exhibitions as characterize "lynching bees." The cannibals of the South Sea Islands roast human beings alive to satisfy hunger. The red Indian of the Western plains tied his prisoner to the stake, tortured him, and danced in fiendish glee while his victim writhed in the flames. His savage, untutored mind suggested no better way than that of wreaking vengeance upon those who had wronged him. These people knew nothing about Christianity and did not profess to follow its teachings; but such primary laws as they had they lived up to. No nation, savage or civilized, save only the United States of America, has confessed its inability to protect its women save by hanging, shooting, and burning alleged offenders.

Finally, for love of country. No American travels abroad without blushing for shame for his country on this subject. And whatever the excuse that passes current in the United States, it avails nothing abroad. With all the powers of government in control; with all laws made by white men, administered by white judges, jurors, prosecuting attorneys, and sheriffs; with every office of the executive department filled by white men—no excuse can be offered for exchanging the orderly administration of justice for barbarous lynchings and "unwritten laws." Our country should be placed speedily above the plane of confessing herself a failure at self-government. This cannot be until Americans of every section, of broadest patriotism and best and wisest citizenship, not only see the defect in our country's armor but take the necessary steps to remedy it. Although lynchings have steadily increased in number and barbarity during the last twenty years, there has been no single effort put forth by the many moral and philanthropic forces of the country to put a stop to this wholesale slaughter. Indeed, the silence and seeming condonation grow more marked as the years go by.

A few months ago the conscience of this country was shocked because, after a two-weeks trial, a French judicial tribunal pronounced Captain Dreyfus guilty. And yet, in our own land and under our own flag, the writer can give day and detail of one thousand men, women, and children who during the last six years were put to death without trial before any tribunal on earth. Humiliating indeed, but altogether unanswerable, was the reply of the French press to our protest: "Stop your lynchings at home before you send your protests abroad."

7

Mary Church Terrell

1863–1954

Mary Church Terrell envisioned that Black success would further racial progress. She was an educator and leader for equality for women and Black people. Her call to action, "Lifting as we climb," was the motto of the National Association of Colored Women, a group she co-founded in 1896 and for which she served as president. She was a co-founder of the National Association for the Advancement of Colored People (NAACP) and remained a steadfast opponent of racial segregation. Well into her eighties, still on the front lines of activism, Terrell helped spearhead the successful effort to desegregate the restaurants and lunch counters of Washington, DC.

Solving the Colored Woman's Problem

World Fellowship of Faiths, August 30, 1933, Chicago, Illinois

---

Colored Women in the United States have more, larger and harder problems to solve than do those of any other racial group. One has only to know the conditions under which they lived for 250 years during slavery and those which obtain today to understand why this is so.

When a small but noble band of women began an agitation in Seneca Falls, New York in 1848, by which colleges were opened to women and numerous reforms inaugurated for the improvement of their condition along all lines, their sisters who groaned in bondage had little reason to ho[pe] that these blessing would ever brighten their crushed and blighted live[s]. For in those days of oppression and despair colored women were not onl[y] refused admission to schools, as a rule, but the law of the States in which the majority lived made it a crime to teach them to read. Not onl[y] could they possess no property, but they did not even own themselves. So pernicious were the customs, so gloomy were their prospects, so fatal the laws only seventy years ago.

But, from the day their fetters were broken and their minds were released from the darkness of ignorance in which they had been held nea[r]ly three hundred years; from the day they could stand in the dignity of womanhood, no longer bond but free till this minute, colored women have forged steadily ahead in the acquisition of knowledge and in the cultivation of these graces of character which make for good. To use a thou[ght] of the illustrious Frederick Douglass, if judged by the depths from which they have come, rather than by the heights to which their more favored sisters have attained, colored women need not hang their heads [i]n shame. The work they have accomplished and the progress they have made will bear favorable comparison, at least with that of more fortunate women from whom the opportunity of acquiring knowledge and the means of self-culture have never been entirely held.

Not only are colored women handicapped on account of their sex, but everywhere in the United States they are baffled and mocked on account of their race. White women both in this country and in England showed what a heavy handicap they considered their sex in their effort to forge ahead by the desperate effort they made to secure the franchise. Particularly did the women of England fight fiercely and frantically to overcome the handicap of sex. I wonder what they would have done if they had had the burden of race as well as of sex to bear. That is exactly the plight in which colored women find themselves in this country today. Not only because they are women, but because they are COLORED women are discouragement and disappointment meeting them at every turn. Trades, pursuits, vocations and opportunities which are opened and offered to women of practically every other race in the United States are withheld from and denied to them.

But, in spite of the opposition encountered and the obstacles opposed, the progress made by colored women along various lines of human endeavor has never been surpassed by that of the women of any other race since the world began. It is very difficult to talk about the subject assigned me, for if a colored woman tells what her group has accomplished as modestly as she possibly can, she is accused of "boasting." "Boasting is the besetting sin of Negroes anyhow," one school of chronic critics declares. But, if a colored woman confines herself exclusively to the difficulties and almost insurmountable obstacles which confront her and block her path to achievement, she is accused of "whining." "Don't you ever get tired of complaining and whining?" she is asked. It is impossible to strike a golden mean. For that reason I have decided to devote about two thirds of my talk tonight to the work which colored women have actually done and the other third to the obstacles and the injustice of which we are the helpless victims.

First I want to tell you what the [*rest of the sentence is cut off*]. Though she was liberated from the most cruel bondage the world has ever seen, penniless, ignorant with no place to lay her head only 70 years ago, so insatiable has been the colored woman's thirst for knowledge and so hard has she worked to satisfy it that there are to day hundreds of colored women who are well educated and some of them hold degrees from the best universities in the land. From Oberlin, Wellesley, Smith, Radcliffe, from the best High Schools and colleges throughout the North, East and West, colored women have graduated with honor and have thus forever settled the question of their intellectual capacity and their worth.

It is a fine thing to want to acquire knowledge for its cultural effect, but it is a far nobler thing to do so to advance the interests of our fellow man. And that is exactly what colored women have done. No sooner had the favored few secured the education advantages which they were able to obtain than they hastened to use their knowledge to enlighten the less fortunate of their racial group. Ever since their emancipation with tireless energy and eager zeal colored women have continuously been prosecuting the work of educating and elevating their race as though upon themselves alone devolved the accomplishment of this herculean task. Of the colored teachers engaged in instructing our youth it is no exaggeration to say that 80% are women.

In the backwoods remote from the conveniences of the city and town, on the plantations reeking with ignorance and vice our women may be found battling with those evils which such conditions always entail. Many a dusky heroine of whom this world will never hear has thus sacrificed her life to her race amid surroundings and in the face of privations which only martyrs can bear. Shirking responsibility has not been a fault with which colored women might truthfully be charged. By banding themselves together in the interest of education and morality and by adopting what they considered the most practical means to this end during the last thirty or forty years colored women have become a tremendous power for good.

Among other things they have been trying to elevate the standards and purify the atmosphere of their homes. They know that so lon[g] as large numbers of any group call that place home in which the air foul, the manners bad and the morals worse, so long will that home b[e] a breeder of vice, a menace to health and the abode of crime. But th[ey] also know that not only upon the head of those who live in these mi[ser]able hovels will the awful consequences of their filth and vice be v[*cut off*]ited, but upon the heads of those who make no effort to stem this tid[e] of disease and sin will vengeance as surely fall.

If the women of the dominant race with all the centuries of ed[u]cation, culture and refinement back of them, with all the wealth of opportunity ever present with them feel the need of a Mother's Congre[ss] so that they may be enlightened concerning the best methods of rearing their children and conducting their homes, how much more do colored from whom the shackles of slavery have but yesterday been stric[*cut off*] need information on these same vital subjects. Therefore, colored wom[en] are trying to solve their problem by establishing Mothers' Congresses on a small scale wherever and whenever they can. They know that the root of many of the evils which militate so seriously against the advancement of the race lies, alas, at their fireside. Homes, more home[s] purer homes, better homes is the text upon which their sermons have been and will be preached.

For years the work of bringing the light of knowledge and the gospel of cleanliness to the benighted women on some of the plantations of the South has been conducted with signal success. Those who have rendered this service have directed their efforts to plantations comprising thousands of acres of land on which live hundreds of colored people, yet in the darkness of ignorance and in the grip of sin miles away from churches and schools. Under the evil influence of certain plantation owners who believe it is more profitable to keep their "hands" as nea[r] the brute creation as possible and through no fault of their own the condition of colored people in some sections of this country is not much better than it was at the close of the Civil War.

These plantation women are given object lessons in the best way to sweep, dust, cook, wash and iron. They are shown how to make their huts more habitable and comfortable by converting dry goods boxes into bureaus, washstands or tables; how to make screens, so as to inculcate lessons of modesty and morality among families. who live in one-room cabins. They are also taught how to clothe and feed their children properly according to their means, what food is the best and most nut[ri]tious for the money and are given other useful information concerning household affairs. Talks on social purity are also given to these mothers who sometimes fall short of their duty, not because they are vicious and depraved, as is so frequently asserted by those who either do not know the facts or willfully distort them, but because they are ignorant and poor.

One of the most useful and successful organizations in the race is the National Association of Colored Women which was founded in 1896 and which now has a membership of about 25,000. In 40 states there are State Federations. Where [there] are no State Federations, there are usually organized clubs affiliated with the national organization.

Magnificent service has been rendered by some of these State Federations. Through their instrumentality unsatisfactory schools have been improved, truant children looked after in those communities whic[h] make no provision for this service, parents and teachers urged to cooperate with each other, rescue and reform work engaged into help unfortunate women and tempted girls [*rest of the sentence is cut off*] to the poor. By the Alabama Federation of Colored Women's Clubs a Reformatory has been built, so that colored boys of tender years need no longer be placed upon the chain gangs to work with hardened criminals or be sent to jail for some minor infraction of the law as has been the case in the past.

Dotted all over the country are institutions of various kinds charitable and others which have either been established or are being maintained by colored women. Among these may be mentioned the Hale Infirmary of Montgomery, Alabama, the Carrie Steel Orphanage of Atlanta, the Reed Orphan Home of Covington, both in the State of Georgia, the Old Folks Home in Memphis, Tennessee, a Home for Aged Colored Women in Pittsburgh, a Colored Orphan's Home in Louisville, Kentucky and othe[r] equally creditable to the women who have founded or are maintain the [*sentence cuts off*].

Many years ago the Phyllis Wheatley Club of New Orleans, Louisiana established a sanitarium with a Training School for Nurses. The conditions which caused the colored women of New Orleans to choose this special field in which to work were such as did obtain and still do obtain in cities and towns practically all over the United States. From the city hospitals colored doctors were excluded altogether—not even being allowed to practice in the colored wards. Colored patients—no matter how ill or well-to-do they were—were not received into the City Hospital at all, unless they were willing to go into the charity wards.

The establishment of this Sanitarium, therefore, answered a variety of purposes. It provided a well-equipped institution to which colored patients might go, if they did not wish to be treated in the charity ward of the City Hospital, and it afforded colored students an excellent opportunity of gaining a practical knowledge of their profession [*sentence cuts off*]. The surgical department was supplied with all the modern appliances. Hu[n]dreds of operations have been performed there, most of which have resulted successfully under the colored surgeon-in-chief.

During an epidemic of yellow fever in New Orleans some years ago Phyllis Wheatley nurses rendered such excellent service that they have been employed by the leading citizens ever since. In short—this Sanitarium with its training School for Nurses which was established by a few energetic, public-spirited, progressive colored women of New Orleans proved to be such a blessing to the city as a whole—without regard to race or color, that the municipal government voted it an annual appropriation of several hundred dollars with which to help defray its expenses.

By some of the clubs Day Nurseries have been established—a charity of which there is imperative need. Thousands of our wage-earning mot[h]ers with large families dependent almost entirely, if not wholly upon them for support, are obliged to leave their children all day, entruste[d] to the care of small brothers and sisters who do not know how to look after them properly, or to some good-natured neighbor who promises much but who does little.

Some of these infants are locked alone in a room from the time th[e] mother leaves in the morning till she returns at night. When one thinks of the slaughter of the innocents which is occurring with pitiless persistency, every day, and reflects upon the multitudes who are maimed for life, or are rendered imbecile by the treatment received during helpless infancy—treatment for which their wage-earning mothers are frequently not responsible—it is evident that by establishing Day Nurseries color[ed] women will render one of the greatest services possible to humanity and their race.

The kindergartens which have been established by colored women li[t]erally fill a long-felt want in the communities in which they are maintained. Nothing lies nearer the heart of colored women than the children[n] and they are trying to promote the welfare of their little ones in ever[y] possible way. They know that the more unfavorable the environment of children, t[*cut off*] more necessary it is that steps be taken to counteract baleful influences upon innocent victims. Therefore, they realize increasingly how imperative it is that they inculcate correct principles and set good examples for their own youth, whose condition in life from the nature of the case is exceedingly hard, whose opportunities are comparatively few and whose temptations are great. Special efforts are being made to reach out after the waifs and strays whose evil natures alone are encouraged to develop and whose better qualities are deadened and dwarfed by the very atmosphere which they breathe.

At the second convention of the National Association of Colored Women which was held in Chicago in 1899 the first president felt that in no better way could she help to solve the problem than by starting a "Kindergarten Fund." She hoped to raise a sufficient fund to send out a Kindergarten Organizer, whose duty it should be to arouse the conscience of colored women to the necessity of saving their children and to establish kindergartens wherever means therefor could be secured. The real solution of the race problem, so far as the group which handicaps and the one which is handicapped is concerned, lies in the children. So long as the children of the two races are allowed to grow up misunderstanding and hating each other, the problem can never be solved. *[hw] Insert here P8 ½ It is surprising [hw]*

[hw] Insert this after "the problem can never be solved and before "I have been trying to show" [hw] It is surprising how many schools have been established by colored women in those sections where the majority of colored people live and where the educational facilities of their youth are often painfully small and few. In such places it is rare that one does not find at least one private school established by a colored women to educate children who would otherwise remain in ignorance.

I have been trying to show what the colored woman has done to work out her own salvation. But there are many things which the colored woman cannot do for herself. She can no more remove the various kinds of injustices of which she is the hapless, helpless victim than a straw can stop Niagara's flow.

One of the most serious problems confronting colored women today is their inability to secure employment in various pursuits in which they are fitted by native ability, education and training successfully to engage. They were handicapped in this way long before the condition obtained which has caused millions to walk the streets in idleness. As a rule colored women will tackle any job they can get. This was strikingly apparent during the World War. Then, in the South, one could see colored women dressed like men lifting heavy burdens, loading and unloading lumber in the railroad yards and doing the heavy, hard work which men usually do and which women of other races could neither be persuaded nor forced to do.

Temporarily, the colored woman's condition was greatly improved by labor conditions brought on by the World War. Pursuits once closed against them hard and fast were then opened unto them for the first tim[e.] But these opportunities for employment have been practically all withdrawn from them, not because they failed to give satisfaction, but because when the soldiers returned from the World War, the necessity for employing colored women no longer existed. Nevertheless, as difficult as it has been and is today for colored women to secure employment, statistics show that according to population there are more wage earners among them then can be found among the women of in any other racial group. To be sure many of the jobs are the kind which are usually spurned by other women, but they enable colored women to earn their living and they do not pick and choo[se.]

The truth of the matter is that with the exception of teaching, sewing and nursing there is practically nothing that a colored woman can ge[t] to do in the United States, no matter how well educated, skillful or prepossessing she may be, or how great her need, unless she is willing to engage in undesirable and distasteful pursuits. The number of young women who can secure positions as typists or stenographers is very small from the nature of the case.

While the women of the dominant race have a variety of trades and pursuits from which they may choose, the woman through whose veins one drop of African blood is known to flow is limited to a pitiful few. As a rule, so overcrowded are the pursuits in which colored women may engage and so poor is the pay in consequence that only the barest livelihood can be eked out by the rank and file. To colored women who are obliged to earn their living, race prejudice which excludes them from most of the gainful occupations and limits them to an unlucrative few means in many cases misery and despair.

The printed report submitted a few years ago of a large wester[n] city throws a flood of light upon this phase of the colored woman's life in this country. It states that owing to prejudice against them on account of their race colored girls are frequently forced to acce[pt] positions in houses of ill fame. "Employment agents do not hesitate to send colored girls to these houses," reads the printed report. "They make the astounding statement that the law does not allow them to send white girls to these immoral places, but they can furnish colored help."

A few years ago Miss Frances Keller, then Director General of the Intermunicipal Committee on Household Research, declared after careful investigation that "colored domestics are more friendless than any other racial group in the North and are subjected to greate[r] dangers that those besetting any other women in this country, except perhaps, the most ignorant of immigrants."

Surely, it is not too much for colored women to hope that those who are interested, not especially in the colored girl, but in the moral welfare of the nation as a whole, will some day realize the necessity of doing everything in their power to create a healthful, wholesome public sentiment in the colored girl's behalf, so that she may have the same chance of earning an honest living as girls of other races enjoy, so long as the womanhood of any race is sacrifice[d] with impunity upon the altar of prejudice, proscription or passion, so long will the womanhood of no race be absolutely secure.

By some of our women the attention of this country is being called to the barbarity of the Convict Lease System which is operated in nearly every State of the South. It is but another form of slavery which in some respects is more cruel and more crushing than the old. Often upon trumped up charges or for offenses which in a civilized community would hardly cause them to be sent to jail, colored men and women too are thrown into dark, damp, disease-breeding cells whose cubic contents are no larger than are those of a good-sized grave. Then they are overworked, underfed and only partially covered with vermin-infested rags.

Scores of children have been born to the women in these camps and they have breathed the polluted atmosphere of those dens of vice and woe from the moment they have uttered their first cry in the world till they have been released from its horrors by death.

So far as lynching is concerned, colored women feel there is little they can do except to appeal to the conscience of the country and urge their white sisters to help them wipe this foul stain upon its escutche[on] away. They believe, however, that much good would be accomplished if th[e] press of the country would continually expose the falsity of the statement that as a rule, colored men are lynched for what is called the "usual crime." Statistics compiled by those who would not falsify in the colored man's favor show that out of every hundred colored men who have been lynched from 75 to 85 have not been accused even by the South of what is maliciously called the "usual crime." And it has been proved again and again that many of those who have been accused of this crime have been absolutely innocent of the charge.

Ever since the colored woman has had a home of her own she has tried to solve her problem by conducting it the best she could. As a home maker, the colored woman deserves an especially bright star in her crown. Some day, perhaps, a genius will arise to pay a fitting, richly-deserved tribute to the poor, ignorant colored mother who ministered so conscientiously and effectively to her children's physical, mental and spiritual needs, as soon as her shackles were snapped.

The education of children immediately after emancipation was [*sentence cut off*] wash tub and stood at the ironing board till midnight, so that she might send her children to school. The world has never seen sacrifices more prodigious and more noble than those made by the colored women of the United States in their dense ignorance and dire poverty, so as to affor[d] their children education facilities of which they themselves had bee[n] deprived.

And it is in the home today that the colored woman finds the problem which i[s] the most difficult for her to solve—the training of her children. It is comparatively easy for a colored mother to impress upon her children the necessity of cultivating their minds, becoming skilled workmen, being honest, energetic and industrious. But, how difficult a thi[ng] it is for a colored mother to inspire her children with home under th[e] existing condition of things in the United States.

As the average mother of the dominant race looks into the innoc[ent] sweet face of her baby, her heart may thrill not only with happiness [*cut off*] the present, but also with joyful anticipations of the future. For, [no] matter how poor she may be, she knows that it is possible for her ba[by] to secure honor, wealth and greatness in any vocation he may choose, if he but possess the ability and the determination to secure them. She knows that if it is in her baby to be great all the exterior cir[cum]stances which can help him to the goal of his ambition,—such as the laws of his country, the public opinion of his countrymen and manifo[ld] opportunities are his without the asking. From his birth he is a kin[g] in his own right and is no suppliant for justice.

But, how striking is the contrast between the emotions of joy [*cut off*] hope which may thrill the heart of the white mother and those which [*cut off*] the soul of her colored sister. As a mother of the proscribed race clasps to her bosom the baby which she loves with an affection as t[en]der and as deep as the white mother bears her child, her heart dare not thrill with joyful anticipations of the future. She knows that [*cut off*] his aspirations are high, as soon as he begins to use his eyes, his ears and to think for himself, the slogan "Thus far shalt thou go and no further," will confront him, wherever he turns, like the handwriting on the wall.

She knows that no matter how skillful his hand, how honest his heart or how dire his need, pursuits of many kinds will be closed against him and that his struggle for existence will be desperate indeed. So rough does the way of her infant appear to many a colored mother, when she thinks of the hardships and humiliations to which he will probably be subjected in his effort to earn his daily bread or to achieve something worth while that instead of thrilling with joy and hope she trembles with apprehension and despair. This picture, though forbitting to look upon, is not overdrawn, as those familiar with the conditions under which the Colored-American lives can abundantly testify.

But, depressing though the situation may be, colored women are not sitting supinely by with drooping heads, weeping eyes and folded hands. Many of them are doing what they can to smooth out the rough roads over which tiny feet that now patter in play may soon stumble and fall. They are urging colored youth to become skillful and reliable in whatever pursuit they intend to engage.

Then, too, colored women believe that their white sisters can do much to help them solve their problems, so they are laying their case squarely and fairly before them, whenever they get a chance. Very few white women know much about the progress, or the problems which colored women have to solve. It is not strange that this is so. Unless colored women do their household work, white women rarely come into personal contact with them at all. As a rule, it is difficult to induce the average white woman's club to allow an intelligent colored person to present facts about his race and the conditions confronting it here, of which most of the members are absolu[te]ly ignorant, but which it is their duty as citizens to know. The majority of newspapers and magazines close their columns to a consideration of the race problem, unless one presents the Colored-American [*sentence cuts off*] of crimes.

There is no doubt whatever that a long step toward the solution of a difficult problem would be taken, if white women could be interested in their colored sister's cause. For that reason colored women are appealing to their large-hearted, broad-minded sisters of the dominant race, of whom there are so many, both to observe themselves and to try to teach their children to observe the lofty principles of justice, liberty, and equality before the law, upon which this government was founded and in which, theoretically, at least, all loyal, American citizens believe.

Colored women beseech their white sisters to help them solve their problem by teaching their children to judge men and women by their intrinsic merit, rather than by the adventitous circumstances of race or color or creed. Colored mothers implore the white parents of the United States to teach their children that, when they grow to manhood and womanhood, if they deliberately prevent their brothers and sisters of a darker hue from earning an honest living by closing the doors of trade against them, the Father of all men will hold them responsible for the crimes which are the result of their injustice and for the human wrecks which the ruthless crushing of hope and ambition always makes.

In the name of the innocence and helplessness of childhood, black as well as white, colored women are appealing to the dominant race to make the future of their boys and girls as bright and as promising as should be that of every child born in a country which owes its very existence to the love of freedom in the human heart.

In various ways colored women have proved indisputably that they intend to work hard to advance the interests of their race. Intelligently and conscientiously a goodly number are studying the questions which deeply and directly affect their race, hoping to find a just and reasonable solution to some of the vexatious problems which confront them.

Against lynching, the Jim Crow Car Laws, the Convict Lease System, cruel discriminations in the various pursuits and trades, they intend to agitate with such force of logic and intensity of soul that those who continue to handicap them will either be converted to principles of righteousness and justice, or be ashamed openly to violate the Golden Rule and flout the very principles upon which this government was built.

Over almost insurmountable obstacles colored women have forged steadily ahead, so that there is scarcely a trade or a profession in which they have not at least worthy representative. In many ways colored women are rendering their race a service whose magnitude and importance it is impossible to estimate or express.

Lifting as they climb, onward and upward they go, struggling, striving and hoping that the door of opportunity will be opened wider unto them before long. With courage born of success which they have achieved in the past and with a keen sense of responsibility which they will continue to assume, they look forward to the future with confidence and hope.

Seeking no favors because of their color, begging for nothing to which they are not entitled as women and which they do not deserve, they knock at the door of justice and ask for an equal chance.

[hw] signifies handwritten material

8

Mary McLeod Bethune

1875-1955

Mary McLeod Bethune, born the daughter of former slaves, emerged as one of the twentieth century's most prominent Black educators—a key advocate for providing educational opportunities for African American children. The school she founded in Daytona, Florida, eventually grew to become Bethune-Cookman University, where she served as president, the first Black woman to hold such a position. Bethune was an influential activist as well as an adviser to President Franklin Delano Roosevelt. She was also the first president of the National Council of Negro Women, an organization she helped foster and that includes over four million members today.

Full Integration—America's Newest Challenge

June 11, 1954, Detroit, Michigan

When first I heard of the Supreme Court decision, I lifted my voice to utter the first inspiration of my heart—and I said,

Let the people praise Thee, O God!
Let ALL the people praise thee.

During this last year of my life, I have had many relationships that are international and far reaching. In every instance I have thought of the people as interesting, beautiful, charming, wonderful. It has never occurred to me that they were strikingly different from myself. I have always found them sharing common experiences which have made our meeting fruitful and memorable. On the local and national scenes this same fact is true. God has enriched me with the power to enjoy people, without labeling them for their color or their national backgrounds. I love people. Inherent in the fundamental principles which were established by our forefathers before they put into words the constitution, there was the essence of democratic living which gave to each man the worthiness of his person and the dignity of his personality. One of the challenges of our new task is that everyone may enjoy self-realization. We belittle our opportunity when we say, "Now is our chance to go to school with white people." That is not the point at all. We want the chance to realize our fullest and best selves in the richest and most inspiring environments under the best guidance that can be made available. Such goodness is not available to all the people when the funds available for such abundance must be allotted for the same thing in fractional proportions. All of our people are free or none are free.

In his last address, which he did not live to speak, Franklin Delano Roosevelt wrote words which were his political testament. He said:

We are faced with the pre-eminent fact that if civilization is to survive, we must cultivate the science of human relationship—the ability of people of all kinds to live together and work together in the same world, at peace.

The World has looked to America for the leadership in that issue of peace through better human relations. The door to the fulfillment of Roosevelt's utterance has just been opened. The challenge is that we must work zealously to discover the ways to put to work our knowledge of the science of human relationships. We know the facts. Now we must practice what we know or we are doomed as a civilization.

The fact that our leaders were able to make this pronouncement portrays our readiness to act upon it. The fruit is ripe to harvest. I pray you then, friends, who among you is prepared to lead up in the harvesting. The challenge of the hour is leadership. Let us discover those who have the abilities and the skills; whose hearts are filled with the understanding and the faith; whose courage is unswerving; whose service motives are worthy of emulation. Let us discover them, I say, and put all that we have in confidence and cooperation and goodwill behind them so that they may be able to lead us to the fullest realization of our goals. All of the challenges to full integration depend upon the kind of education and ground work we do from this point on. We are often reminded by leaders outside the field of education, that the educative process is slow. H. G. Wells warned our world that if our processes of training did not change, our civilization was already doomed. The works of science and technology have far surpassed our understanding. Human beings change slowly. Some of us still recite the age-old adage:

Be not the first by whom the new is tried
Nor yet the last to lay the old aside.

But in the words of a newer philosophy,

Time makes ancient good uncouth.

We must be upward and doing if we would keep abreast with truth. So it is today my earnest plea that we work cooperatively and with great precision toward the dissemination of the truths that will undergird the realization of a full integration. What are the facts? Who can best give them to the people? When and where are the best places? What organized groups already have the platforms and the facilities that we need? It all means that we lay aside our own bigotries and littleness and with an open mind prepare the people to accept the new responsibilities. Let us pray for the illumination of our minds and our hearts and then let us set to work with a master will to achieve.

The tools are in our hands. All the people love art, literature, music, for in them is full release and harmony. They are the therapies for wounded minds and broken spirits. The world is hungry for the love which can be brought to the people through the avenues of life. They turn away anger, subside fears, and kill evils.

You must work too to discover the common needs which may become the common tasks of many people. You know what they are, but you have not taken time to put the variety of peoples at work together upon them. These now are your responsibilities. More than ever now we need to know what the gifts and powers of the people are so that we may use them for the common good.

What Does American Democracy Mean to Me

America's Town Meeting of the Air, November 23, 1939, New York, New York

---

Democracy is for me, and for 12 million black Americans, a goal towards which our nation is marching. It is a dream and an ideal in whose ultimate realization we have a deep and abiding faith. For me, it is based on Christianity, in which we confidently entrust our destiny as a people. Under God's guidance in this great democracy, we are rising out of the darkness of slavery into the light of freedom. Here my race has been afforded [the] opportunity to advance from a people 80 percent illiterate to a people 80 percent literate; from abject poverty to the ownership and operation of a million farms and 750,000 homes; from total disfranchisement to participation in government; from the status of chattels to recognized contributors to the American culture.

As we have been extended a measure of democracy, we have brought to the nation rich gifts. We have helped to build America with our labor, strengthened it with our faith and enriched it with our song. We have given you Paul Lawrence Dunbar, Booker T. Washington, Marian Anderson and George Washington Carver.

But even these are only the first fruits of a rich harvest, which will be reaped when new and wider fields are opened to us.

The democratic doors of equal opportunity have not been opened wide to Negroes. In the Deep South, Negro youth is offered only one-fifteenth of the educational opportunity of the average American child. The great masses of Negro workers are depressed and unprotected in the lowest levels of agriculture and domestic service, while the black workers in industry are barred from certain unions and generally assigned to the more laborious and poorly paid work. Their housing and living conditions are sordid and unhealthy. They live too often in terror of the lynch mob; are deprived too often of the Constitutional right of suffrage; and are humiliated too often by the denial of civil liberties. We do not believe that justice and common decency will allow these conditions to continue.

Our faith in visions of fundamental change as mutual respect and understanding between our races come in the path of spiritual awakening. Certainly there have been times when we may have delayed this mutual understanding by being slow to assume a fuller share of our national responsibility because of the denial of full equality. And yet, we have always been loyal when the ideals of American democracy have been attacked. We have given our blood in its defense—from Crispus Attucks on Boston Commons to the battlefields of France. We have fought for the democratic principles of equality under the law, equality of opportunity, equality at the ballot box, for the guarantees of life, liberty and the pursuit of happiness. We have fought to preserve one nation, conceived in liberty and dedicated to the proposition that all men are created equal. Yes, we have fought for America with all her imperfections, not so much for what she is, but for what we know she can be.

Perhaps the greatest battle is before us, the fight for a new America: fearless, free, united, morally re-armed, in which 12 million Negroes, shoulder to shoulder with their fellow Americans, will strive that this nation under God will have a new birth of freedom, and that government of the people, for the people and by the people shall not perish from the earth. This dream, this idea, this aspiration, this is what American democracy means to me.

9

Nannie Helen Burroughs

1879–1961

Nannie Helen Burroughs founded and served as president of the National Training School for Women and Girls in Washington, DC, which had the motto "We Specialize in the Wholly Impossible." She first came to prominence at the age of twenty-one on the basis of her speech "How the Sisters Are Hindered from Helping," presented at the National Baptist Convention (NBC) in 1900. She subsequently helped found and then led NBC's Woman's Auxiliary for six decades. Throughout her life, Burroughs fought sex and racial discrimination against the Black community and rose above the color consciousness within the Black community, an insidious vestige of slavery. She was active in voting rights and political empowerment.

Black Women and Reform

August 1915

Burroughs's remarks from "Votes for Women: A Symposium by Leading Thinkers of Colored Women," held in Washington, DC, as published in the August 1915 issue of The Crisis *(vol. 10, no. 4).*

The Negro Church means the Negro woman. Without her, the race could not properly support five hundred churches in the whole world. Today they have 40,000 churches in the United States. She is not only a great moral and spiritual asset, but she is a great economic asset. I was asked by a southern white woman who is an enthusiastic worker for "votes for (white) women," "What can the Negro woman do with the ballot?" I asked her, "What can she do without it?" When the ballot is put into the hands of the American woman the world is going to get a correct estimate of the Negro woman. It will find her a tower of strength of which poets have never sung, orators have never spoken, and scholars have never written. Because the black man does not know the value of the ballot, and has bartered and sold his most valuable possession, it is no evidence that the Negro woman will do the same. The Negro woman, therefore, needs the ballot to get back, by the wise use of it, what the Negro man has lost by the misuse of it. She needs it to ransom her race. A fact worthy of note is that in every reform in which the Negro woman has taken part, during the past fifty years, she has been as aggressive, progressive and dependable as those who inspired the reform or led it. The world has yet to learn that the Negro woman is quite superior in bearing moral responsibility. A comparison with the men of her race, in moral issues, is odious. She carries the burdens of the Church, and of the school and bears a great deal more than her economic share in the home. Another striking fact is that the Negro woman carries the moral destiny of two races in her hand. Had she not been the woman of unusual moral stamina that she is, the black race would have been made a great deal whiter, and the white race a great deal blacker during the past fifty years. She has been left a prey for the men of every race, but in spite of this, she has held the enemies of Negro female chastity at bay. The Negro woman is the white woman's as well as the white race's most needed ally in preserving an unmixed race. The ballot, wisely used, will bring to her the respect and protection that she needs. It is her weapon of moral defense. Under present conditions, when she appears in court in defense of her virtue, she is looked upon with amused contempt. She needs the ballot to reckon with men who place no value upon her virtue, and to mould healthy public sentiment in favor of her own protection.

What the Negro Wants Politically

circa 1928

You heard about the election.

The Democratic Party is pretty well banged up, the Republican Party is all set up. It was a Landslide! It was a political miracle! It is a waste of time trying to explain how it happened. It got started and nobody could stop it.

Now that a grand and glorious victory has been achieved in the name of Righteousness, let no group or race try to hog the victory. "We cannot say that this great victory is attributed to any one source. Take your share."

Of course the "Wiseacres" will say, "I told you so," and then proceed to tell how it all happened. The job-seekers will say, "I did it. With my bow and arrow, I killed 'Cock Smith.'" So over against what they put down as the "How + the why" please do not allow them to overlook the real factors that gave to the Republican Party an unprecedented victory.

1st The strength of the platform

2d The superior fitness and sanity of the candidates

3d The efficiency of the Hoover organization

4th The perfection of the radio

5th The power of the press

6th The service of the "Spell-Binders"

7th The horse sense of the electorate

8th The Democratic Party that unwittingly ran a showman instead of a statesman. He woke them up and brought them out.

9th And above all, millions of women who talked Herbert Hoover up and talked Al Smith out.

Despite the fact that the campaign was begun on an elevated platform from which the American people were to discuss their ideals, hopes, and dreams in terms and promises of prosperity, projects, protection and peace, it ended in a fight on the sidewalks of New York, over rum, race, and religion.

The injection of the race issue into the campaign raised two questions—

First—Did many Negroes bolt the Republican Party? No. It is true that a larger number of colored people voted the Democratic ticket this year than at any time since they have had the franchise. There were two reasons:

(a) The race is actually chafing under national injustice and the Republican Party is justly charged with some "sins of omission" and dereliction of a patriotic duty. (b) Tammany Hall helped finance the Democratic Party, and Tammany Hall bids for Negro votes because it needs them and it knew that in order to help the Democratic Party win, they would have to get a large defection of Negro votes. They did not get the large defection and Tammany Hall was kicked from the side walk into the sewer and the Democratic Party, which is the "solid South" was smashed to pieces and "all the king's horses and all the king's men will never put the 'solid South' together again." The Republican Party cannot sweep the country without the Negro's vote. Oh, yes, it is said, they can but try it—"It can't be did."

Secondly—What does the Negro want politically? He wants his rights as an American citizen and not simply jobs for a few politicians. That's what he wants.

Thirdly—He wants general relief from demoralizing evils, rather than personal rewards for party fealty.

He will, therefore, call upon the Republican Party to—

Enforce the Constitution and all of its amendments.

Compel the Interstate Commission to make the railroads operating in "Jim Crow" states provide equal accommodations for the races on the trains and in the waiting rooms. The railroads are guilty of highway robbery. They charge Negroes firstclass fares and give them cattle accommodations.

Break up segregation in the Departments at Washington.

Appoint a National, Non-Partisan, Bi-racial Welfare Commission whose duty it will be to make unbiased investigations and practical suggestions that will give relief from: (a) Disfranchisement. (b) Unequal accommodations in travel. (c) Segregations in Federal Departments. (d) Race discrimination in Civil Service appointments. (e) Discrimination in relief work in times of floods and disasters. (f) Unequal opportunity, in times of peace, to learn the arts of war in army, navy, and aerial service.

Appoint two colored women, specialists, to work in the Childrens Bureau and the Woman's Bureau, the former for child welfare and the latter for industrial and economic welfare among women. Both positions would require highly trained women and their work among colored women and children would parallel the work that is being done by the heads of these two bureaus, primarily for white children and women and incidentally, for colored children and women. Conditions and needs among the children and women of the Negro race justify these appointments. Politicians need not try to further deceive the Republican Party by trying to make them believe that a recordership, registership, ministership, assistantship, or any of the usual "sop" appointments will ever be accepted by the Negro race as substitutes for simple justice and equal opportunity.

At the proper time and the proper way the men and women who are seeking relief for the masses from the injustices herein listed, will prepare their case, secure the backing of every Negro organization, political and non-political, and lay their petition before Congress and the Chief Executive and seek and work for redress.

In preparation for more effective action, the Negroes throughout the country should keep all of their clubs in tact, hold regular meetings, carry on a campaign of education and enlightenment and thereby build up a vigorous morale and be ready for the "fire-works" four years from now.

The best advice to give our people, politically, is organize and keep organized, study men and measures, put down every "sin of omission, or commission", get every congressman's number—know what he is saying and how he is voting, and "meet him at Philippi." At the same time do not forget to repudiate all of the Negro political leaders who drag around begging for jobs for themselves and never contending for justice and opportunities for the race. They are more responsible for our political undoing than the whites. Do not let them out.

There is one thing that we do not want to see again—"Jim Crow" National Republican Headquarters—We had three. Ye gods. What [*illegible*] a duplication of machinery, a place for Negroes to disagree on everything from the personnel and the modus operandi to the postage stamp and sheet of paper, which they cannot get without an order.

We are calling upon the Republican Party to break up segregation in the Departments and in the same breath we ask the National Republican Committee—the machine which puts the Party in power—[*illegible*] us three "Jim Crow" headquarters. "Consistency, thou art a jewel."

Four years are not too long to work and wait. The smashing victory in Ky was due to the Negro vote. The breaking up of the "solid South," regardless of whether we believe it now or not, and the building up of a two-party government in the South is a move in the right direction. As long as the South remains a government of white men, by white men, and for white men instead of a government of the people, by the people, and for the people, the Negro will never enjoy his rights as an American citizen nor receive anything like just consideration in the distribution of funds from the taxes which he pays for public education, protection and general welfare.

With the ballot in his hand he has a weapon of defense, protection, and expression. Both parties will need his vote and he will learn to use it wisely.

Regardless of the cost to the Negro race of a few offices which we have held in the South as political rewards for party fealty, the gain to the race and to the Negroes of the South in a two-party government will be worth transcendently more than all the jobs which are given a few Negro politicians who have not been able and who would never be able to build up a Republican Party in the South and thereby deliver their race from political bondage. Only one Negro, [*illegible*] Church has really been able to build up a fighting organization.

The only hope for a semblance of even handed justice for the Southern Negro is in a two-party government. It is an American ideal and without two parties this country is not a democracy. It is half democracy and half oligarchy. On with the two-party government in the South or out with some of the representatives in Congress who ride into office on the backs of Negroes whom they use as political ponies.

Since the Negro vote helped the Republican Party win the 1928 victory, the question has been asked again and again, what does it profit the Negro to give his vote to keep the Republican Party in power? Here is the answer, With all its faults it is the better party. In this campaign the Negro voted against Democratic ideals for his race, against tampering with the Constitution, against an increase of the emigration quota, against tinkering with the tariff, against a man who is not qualified to be president of the United States. The Negro simply voted for the strongest platform and the better qualified man.

The Negro gave his vote to Herbert Hoover, because Mr. Hoover stood four-square on the strong platform of the Republican Party and pledged equal opportunities to all, regardless of faith or race. The American Negro asks nothing more and will be satisfied with nothing less.

10

Lucy Diggs Slowe

1885–1937

Lucy Diggs Slowe was the valedictorian of her 1908 graduating class at Howard University. She became the school's first female dean of women. In addition to education, her advocacy for Black advancement included economic empowerment. She was a founder of the National Council of Negro Women and the National Association of College Women.

The Negro and the New Order: Summary of Speech Delivered by Lucy D. Slowe, Dean of Women, Howard University

Mu-So-Lit Club, March 19, 1933, Washington, DC

In the last two weeks America has gone from a representative form of government to a dictatorship. This change was accompanied by no bloodshed as happened when Russia passed from the Czarist regime to the Communistic form of government, nor such as happened in Italy when Mussolini established the Fascist government, nor such as happened in Germany when Hitler dethroned the Republican form of government. In spite of Americans' love of democracy, they have given to President Roosevelt unprecedented power without serious objection from any considerable group because the economic situation in our country demand that somebody be given absolute authority. It is true that the authority granted to President Roosevelt can be taken from him when the electorate sees fit to do so, but to all intents and purposes America is now under the control of a dictator.

A few months ago, in the heat of the political campaign, many of us were loudly proclaiming that we belonged to the Democratic party. From our words and actions we seemed to believe that it was quite important that we bear one or the other of these labels. Subsequent events, however, have demonstrated to us that when our economic security is threatened it does not make very much difference what political party we belong to. We are all in the same boat and we are all forced to find common measures of security. Therefore, when President Roosevelt produced plans which seemed to be designed to give us greater economic security, Republicans, Democrats, Socialists and what not got behind his program and were glad to do so.

The events of the last few months ought to mean a great deal to the Negro so far as his political philosophy is concerned. He ought to see that after all the fundamental question for him in America today is the same fundamental question for every other American citizen; namely, that of economic security. Furthermore, he ought to see that he must secure this by the same means and techniques that other American citizens must use to secure it. He ought to see that his welfare is wrapped up with the welfare of every other insecure group; and that is not only to his advantage, but it is absolutely necessary for his survival, that he join hands with other groups to secure the means by which he shall live.

It is my opinion that the Negro has placed entirely too much dependence in the past in what might be termed "inspirational" leadership. He has listened to numerous speeches from so-called leaders who have had nothing concrete to offer him in the way of helping him solve his problems. Sometimes these leaders have been self-appointed and sometimes they have been foisted upon the Negro, by the people outside of the race. Unfortunately, these so-called leaders have spoken the language of their masters and that language has not had for its purpose the building up of independent individuals in the Negro race. Some of these leaders have gone so far as to condemn any Negro who attempted to question their philosophy or their words, and have tried to make Negroes believe that is was sacrilegious to criticize them. It is a very interesting fact in history that nearly all progress has been made by those persons who had the temerity to criticize and to question the leaders of dominant groups.

Since the troubles of the Negro, in my judgment, are almost entirely economic, it is necessary that he shall develop within the race a large number of men and women who are experts in collective information related to his economic welfare and in interpreting that information where it will do the most good. It is necessary that he develop within the race a large number of experts in political science, in sociology and in every other field that has to do with his economic security. These experts ought to be spokesmen for the Negro and what they say ought to be based upon scientific inquiry, scientifically interpreted. It is my opinion, that the day is past when anything much can be gained from having one or two so-called spokesmen speak to the world for the Negro; and in the new order of things it seems to me that facts, handled by people who know what to do with them, must speak and act for our race. This has been the procedure for all other groups who have been able to solve their problem; and I see no reason why we should expect to solve ours in any way different from the way in which other people solve theirs. We do not need in the new order so many "inspirational" leaders, but we do need men and women who have enough training to collect information and enough courage to use that information where it should be used.

Education and Race Relations

August 19, 1931, Chautauqua, New York

Someone has said that education is the inflicting of prejudices of an older generation upon the unexpected present generation. Although this is an exaggerated statement, yet it contains a great deal of truth, particularly in its application to race relations. Let me examine a few typical examples of race attitudes:

A few months ago I was on my way to the home of a friend to dinner. Being a little late I hailed a taxi cab driven by an Irishman and asked him to go as rapidly as the law would allow. When we pulled up to the house, he naively asked, "Are you late for work?" So far as he was concerned, only white people could live in a home like that which I was entering and I, being a Negro would be going there only in the capacity of a servant. He probably did not know that there were any Negroes in the world who occupied any other status than that of serving white people.

A friend of mine, making a trip from Washington to Detroit, went into the diner on the train and was placed at the table with a man of the white race, very intelligent and cultured in appearance.

As soon as she was seated, he dramatically jumped up from the table, stalked out of the diner, exclaiming that he would be damned before he would eat at the table with a nigger. He did not wait to find out whether she was offensive or inoffensive in manner; it was enough for him to know that she was a Negro. That stimulus caused him to lose his good manner, his temper, his peace of mind, and an intelligent attitude toward a new situation.

A third typical attitude was exhibited by an official of one of our large Universities in the North, for these attitudes are by no means confined to the ignorant classes. A woman of my acquaintance wished to enter her daughter in a certain University. The girl had the necessary academic qualifications, but the Dean of the school without seeing her sent her mother the following letter:

"While we could not exclude a qualified student on account of her color, I do feel that a colored girl would be very unhappy situated in this college since she necessarily would be very much isolated socially.———In view of these facts, we strongly recommend that you do not enroll your daughter in———University."

Since these three examples taken from three different levels of American life represent the usual every day reactions of American white people to American negroes, it is logical to inquire how these people developed these attitudes. Is racial antipathy or a feeling of racial superiority born in people or do they acquire it themselves?

Fortunately, for those of us engaged in the work of educating the young we know that racial attitudes are not inherited but are acquired. This being the case, we know that these acquired attitudes can be modified, changed, eradicated; and better still that they need not be developed. Bruno Lasker in his studies "Race Attitudes in Children" has come to the conclusion that children brought up in an environment free from racial prejudices do not acquire it.

One the other hand we know how easy it is not only to acquire it but how assiduously some people cultivate it in their children. It is no exaggeration to say that all over America today the majority of white People are either directly or indirectly teaching their children that white people as a group are superior to colored people as a group.

This being the case, it is not surprising to find race proscription in every division of American life, civic, political, industrial and even religious. The inflicting of the thoughtless beliefs of older people on the young, the building up on them the belief that all Negroes are inferior to any white person has been so successful that the very word Negro connotes to most white people an ignorant, shuffling, unkept being, fit for menial tasks and nothing more.

Out of this popular but thoughtless conception of Negroes have grown all sorts of practices in American life as that life touches the daily interests of the Negro. If he wished to travel in his native land, he must ride in the South in separate cars regardless of his culture or his means. Almost no hotel run for the accommodation of the general public will accommodate him. It matters not whether it be situated North or South. He is required to pay taxes, to support the government in time of peace and to bear arms in time of war, but in several Southern states he may not cast his ballot for those who are to spend their share of the taxes.

Even before the present industrial depression he was the last man hired and the first fired. The whole range of commercial and industrial opportunities above the level of porter and janitor have been consistently closed to him. In many places, the so-called house of God in which white people worship does not welcome him. I have heard of several places where Negroes take holy communion in the basement, while white people take it upstairs.

If these conditions do exist and you and I know they do, can we out of them build for the future in America a civilization characterized by respect for human personality and by high standards of fair play, of sympathy, justice and open-mindedness. Can our civilization endure upon any other basis? I am as much concerned with the sort of characters that we are developing in white boys and girls by our present race attitudes as I am in those of the boys and girls of my own people. When we realize that character is the result of one's daily acts as well as the results of one's environment in a very large degree, we should examine with very great care the actions of most Americans toward colored people. Can we be unfair, cruel and inhuman to any man without having our characters sullied? Dr. Felix Adler, who has contributed so much to American education through the Society of Ethical Culture, has pointed out the way for us toward better race relations through education. His philosophy concerns itself with man's relationship to man; with his attitude toward his fellow-man. He believes that every man must have opportunity to develop his latent gifts assisted by his associates who recognize him as kindred spirit.

In a recent interview he said: "We have stood for the relief of the oppressed, not merely that the downtrodden may take a deeper breath, but because the state of being oppressed and the state of the oppressor, too, are hostile to the development of the worth that is latent in man."

It is because I believe that racial antipathy cultivated as it has been in America will lead to the disintegration of American character that I urge upon homes, schools and churches a concerted effort at education for racial appreciation instead of education for racial hatred. How is it to be done? First, we must set up worthy objectives in the education of our youth, and make a concerted effort in our schools to achieve these objectives. If, then, we wish to change the prevailing attitude of American white people toward the Negro, we must do three fundamental things:

We must make individuals more sensitive to the claims of justice in dealing with people regardless of race. It is my belief that we are in grave danger of a complete moral collapse in America, because we put such a low evaluation upon injustice when it concerns Negroes. It is easy to lose one's sense of fair dealing unless one exercises it unceasingly. Justice cannot be selective it must be **co-extensive** with humanity. It is an easy step from taking away the ballot from Negroes by subterfuge and unjust law to taking it away from white people by bribery and trickery. Justice cannot be selective; if it exists for all.

We must set up opportunities for getting authentic information, and for counteracting misunderstanding in matters affective the two races. If in schools the contribution of the Negro to American history could be studies, what a different point of view many Americans would have. The intelligent open-minded way of finding out what all classes of Negroes think and do should be our mode of breaking down prejudice, of dissipating ignorance. Such books as Woodson's "The Negro in Our History," Moton's "What the Negro Thinks," Charles S. Johnson's "The Negro in American Civilization" would undoubtedly shed light on the historical and sociological background of this group of citizens and assist us in understanding why they are as they are.

Moreover such studies would tend to make us realize that economic and political conditions are more potent factors in fixing the characteristics of any group than accident of color of birth.

Open-mindedness which comes with opinion based on facts rather than on feelings is as greatly needed in studying race relations as it is in making a new experiment in chemistry.

We need also to realize that every racial group has some qualities and achievements which are of universal value and therefore transcend the bounds of race. In America our cultural life is richer for the music of such Negroes as Burleigh, Dett, Hayes and others; our literature is richer for the poetry of Paul Laurence Dunbar, James Weldon Johnson, Countee Cullen, Claude McKay, Langston Hughes and others. Appreciation through knowledge of these contributions will break down the stereotyped Negro and bring us to realize that many, many individuals with various talents make up this group. This realization will compel us to deal with these individuals on the basis of their worth, and will force us to discontinue thinking of them as a group, legislative for them as group, looking down on them as a group.

In looking, then, at this whole question of race relations we are looking at something which needs our finest thought. The sort of training which has produced racial antagonism in the United States has produced it throughout the world. Race hatred based upon ignorance and emotion has led and will lead to war, to strife, to injustice, to selfishness and to the destruction of all that is ignoble in human beings. We owe it to our children to include in their subject of study books which do justice to the best that has been produced by all the peoples of the world. Interracial conferences and commissions are doing some notable work, but our whole system of education and modes of thought concerning the Negro in America must be changed if this difficult problem is to be solved. It seems to me that the children of the next generation should be better prepared to deal with this question than their fathers and mothers are and we who are interested in seeing the finest qualities of character developed must make it our task to set up right educational opportunities.

Bruno Lasker has very wisely said: "Generation after Generation of children are given the stones of fictitious stereotypes when they ask for the bread of knowledge; children of all races and nationalities made potential cannon fodder of future wars because they are not permitted to develop in themselves those qualities of mind that make for a sense of fair play, for mutual appreciation, for mental flexibility in response to changing situations. It is to these children, burdened with the material costs of past wars and with the inheritance of limiting social attitudes that society owes its greatest unacknowledged debt."

In the interest of all the people of our land and country; in the interest of saving our moral integrity; in the interest of the preservation and improvement of our social order we should deal with Race Relations in a scientific and dispassionate manner; the intellect must replace the emotions in dealing with this subject and this calls for the thought of our finest educators.

11

Ella Baker

1903–1986

Ella Baker is best known for her work as the key strategist for the Student Nonviolent Coordinating Committee (SNCC), although she played central roles in the broader Civil Rights Movement, working with the Southern Christian Leadership Conference and the NAACP. Baker was the highest-ranking woman in the NAACP and among its most effect organizers, often working behind the scenes in local communities across the South. The young people of SNCC revered her as *fundi*, from the Swahili word indicating intergenerational skills building and leadership.

Address at SNCC Conference

December 1, 1963, Washington, DC

I suppose it must be an indication of my growing old, I actually get affected by such applause. I almost lose my sense of balance and want to sort of act like a female and cry. I don't know whether that's good or bad for me.

I had not anticipated having anything to say, and I think it's very gracious of Jim [Forman] to not only call on me, but to indicate that what SNCC is, is the result of what the people are who are in SNCC. And SNCC if it is anything different from any of the rest of the groups that have come on the scene, I hope is different in two respects in particular: one is, it is concerned with not the development of a leader, but the development of leadership. And there's a lot of difference between the development of single individuals as leaders and the development of leadership, with leadership concepts, leadership goals, leadership methods that people can follow after we have moved on, and we must all move on from one point to the other.

I think it's different in that respect; it's also different in the respect that it goes into the hardcore areas and identifies very closely with people. It works with people. It lives with people. And it has had to do this especially in the areas where it worked, because there they found—and we all know this, if we hadn't known it, we should know it—that in order to get people in deep areas of the South to move, to even act in their own behalf, they have to first be given a feeling of confidence in you, and then this gives them the feeling of confidence so that they can break through the years of fear and suppression that they have experienced. And this I think SNCC has done a good pioneering job in, setting the pace for others to follow.

I think if we are to move forward, as we can move forward, we have to also combine that other thing that I hope will become very unique with us and which was conceived in the beginning, namely that we bring to bear on the problems of race, the problems of human suffering, not only our own emotional righteous indignation with the situation, but we use the full capacities of our thinking and our minds and others' minds to actually think through and to chart programs that people can respond to and programs that have basic effect on changing the system so people can live instead of just exist.

I wish that we had time tonight, not tonight, but certainly during the conference to analyze further that which Bob Moses set before us this morning. And if we don't do it now, we've got to do it as a staff, because we have reached the point that the old line methods of just getting out in a demonstration just for the sake of demonstrating is far from being enough. And we've got to find ways in which to involve people at many different levels. And we've got to find ways in which to evaluate our own selves in respect to the movement. Frequently we don't find time to look at ourselves. And this is one of the reasons why, today, when Mr. [James] Baldwin made the statement to the effect that the white man, in order to find his role in the movement, he would have to forget that he's white. I think we also have to forget that we are Negroes as such. But we forget that only in terms of not trying to feel that the white fellow who comes into our movement has to come by us. Now I can understand, as we grow in our own strength and as we flex our muscles of leadership, and flex our muscles that have come from seeing how effective we are, we can begin to feel that the other fellow should come through us. But this is not the way to create a new world. We can only create a new world out of a commonness of purpose and a decent respect for all the people who are helping to contribute to it.

I don't think we need to be afraid. Certainly we don't need to be afraid of being taken over, if we know where we're going, know why we are going there, and then know how we're going to get there.

I suppose if I'd wanted to speak, I could have been shorter. But since I didn't want to speak—no, I don't think I should, Jim, no, I got some other things we can talk about later—but maybe before the conference is over we can have an opportunity to talk some. But certainly we ought to begin to think very seriously about the directions in which we are going and assume the responsibility that has been laid on our shoulders as a result of the fact that, whether we like it or not, we have been able to pioneer in a direction that had not been pioneered before.

When you talked about a movement on Mississippi, you called it MOM. I remember those days. And I remember the fact that we didn't move on Mississippi when we thought we were going to move on Mississippi. But I also remember that you didn't forget to dream, that you didn't forget it, and that when Bob Moses went down into McComb, Mississippi, and inspired such people as Brenda Travis, who is here somewhere—I don't know whether she is here or not in the audience—but inspired the high school students of McComb, Mississippi. And when out of this came some other people, and when you began to come to the conferences, and no longer were there ten or twelve people who were on the staff, but there were twenty, and there were thirty, and then there's now over a hundred people, people who come to the staff because they feel it offers some opportunity to find some greater meaning in life, and an opportunity to help provide . . .

[*break in tape*]

He said, "I been wondering what keeps you going?" And afterwards I thought about it myself. What is it that keeps people who have been going as long as I have trying to keep going? I think one of the things that keeps one going is a faith in human beings. Basically I believe human beings want to live in a decent world. Basically I believe that the young people of today really are out to create that kind of world. And if I didn't believe that there would be no virtue in my living, because I cannot see any virtue even in using one's creative instinct, one's creative capacities, if we cannot create a world in which people can live, then we haven't done anything.

When I was much younger, I used to make speeches that were much better rounded, and one of them had to do with this subject: that to penetrate the mystery of life and to perfect the mastery of life were the twin goals of great living. At that time, and I suppose I can still say now, we have done much in the direction of penetrating the mystery of life. With all this equipment we have around us, it is part of the penetration of the mystery of life. And when we hear about the Telstar and all of the marvelous things of science—the computer machines and all of these things—this is part of the penetration of the mystery of life. But where we have failed, and failed so woefully, is the perfection of the mastery of life. And there can be no perfection of the mastery of life until we have learned that human beings are human beings worthy of the dignity and respect wherever they are, irrespective of who they are.

And as Jim Forman pointed out today, what we think of others, we can so easily become. And this is a danger for us. When we look at these irrational people, and we know they're irrational, when we see as I happened to have seen, about the 31st of October, four young white men who trailed us from Natchez, Mississippi, to Port Gibson, and then jumped out of their car and vented their spleen on Bruce Payne, a young graduate student at Yale University. Why did they find it necessary to do this? Why do they find it necessary to take out their venom on somebody else? Because somewhere, somehow, they have been fooled.

And you and I know a great deal of why they have been fooled. And they have been fooled and made to feel that they had something of value in being white. And then deep down inside of them they knew this was not true, that they knew that just being white was not enough, and so they are confused and they don't know where to turn. And so when we gaze upon these people, we gaze upon them not with a sense of despising them, or even rejecting them, or being overcritical of them, but being understanding of what has made them into what they are. And part of our task, as I see it, is to help them to see that they can be something other than that, and I don't know whether it comes through nonviolence or not, but it certainly comes through an understanding of your own value, so that you do not feel it necessary to lord it over somebody else just because you have the opportunity to do so. These things may be very elementary, but I think they are basic to what we become and how well we carry the torch that has been handed to us.

I am glad to see so many people in SNCC that I don't know them. But I do hope, that whoever we are, and wherever we are, that we will continue to think in terms of the fact that what we do in SNCC is not for the development of SNCC as a big, powerful organization, nor for getting headlines. But we do this because we believe that it is necessary to change the political and social system of Alabama, Georgia, Mississippi, and yes to change the political and social system in respect to the entire country. So that when we say we have a democratic country and when we claim that we're a nation for the people and by the people, it will truly be a people's nation and a people's government. And this can only be if the people themselves understand how valuable they are, and understand what it takes to become a nation of the people, for the people, and by the people. And we have the opportunity to help the people understand this, and understand it in a way and in a depth that we perhaps haven't even begun to find the final depth for. But I think this is an opportunity and I'm glad that I'm here tonight.

The three years from '60 to '63, out of my fifty-odd years, seems to me to be the best years of my life. I hope I have three more to be with you.

The Black Woman in the Civil Rights Struggle

Institute of the Black World, December 31, 1969,
Atlanta, Georgia

I think that perhaps because I have existed much longer than you and have to some extent maintained some degree of commitment to a goal of full freedom that this is the reason Vincent Harding invited me to come down as an exhibit of what might possibly be the goal of some of us to strive toward—that is, to continue to identify with the struggle as long as the struggle is with us.

I was a little bit amazed as to why the selection of a discussion on the role of black women in the world. I just said to Bernice Reagon that I have never been one to feel great needs in the direction of setting myself apart as a woman. I've always thought first and foremost of people as individuals . . . [but] wherever there has been struggle, black women have been identified with that struggle. During slavery there was a tremendous amount of resistance in various forms. Some were rather subtle and some were rather shocking. One of the subtle forms was that of feigning illness. . . . One of the other forms of resistance which was perhaps much more tragic and has not been told to a great extent is the large number of black women who gave birth to children and killed them rather than have them grow up as slaves. There is a story of a woman in Kentucky who had borne thirteen children and strangled each of them with her own hands rather than have them grow up as slaves. Now this calls for a certain kind of deep *commitment* and *resentment. Commitment* to freedom and deep *resentment* against slavery.

I would like to divide my remaining comments into two parts. First, the aspect that deals with the struggle to get into the society, the struggle to be a part of the American scene. Second, the struggle for a different kind of society. The latter is the more radical struggle. In the previous period, the period of struggling to be accepted, there were certain goals, concepts, and values such as the drive for the "Talented Tenth." That, of course, was the concept that proposed that through the process of education black people would be accepted in the American culture and they would be accorded their rights in proportion to the degree to which they qualified as being persons of learning and culture. . . .

[There was] an assumption that those who were trained were not trained to be part of the community, but to be leaders of the community. This carried with it another false assumption that being a leader meant that you were separate and apart from the masses, and to a large extent people were to look up to you, and that your responsibility to the people was to represent them. This means that the people were never given a sense of their own values. . . . Later, in the 1960s, a different concept emerged: the concept of the right of the people to participate in the decisions that affected their lives. So part of the struggle was the struggle toward intellectualism [which] so often separated us so far from the masses of people that the gulf was almost too great to be bridged.

The struggle for being a part of the society also led to another major phase of the civil rights struggle. That was the period in which legalism or the approach to battling down the barriers of racial segregation through the courts which was spearheaded by the National Association for the Advancement of Colored People. . . . We moved from the question of equal educational opportunity in terms of teachers' salaries into another phase: equality in travel accommodations. . . . One of the young persons who was part of the first efforts to test [segregated travel] was Pauli Murray. Pauli Murray and I were part of a committee that was organized to try to go into the South to test Jim Crow in bus travel. But the decision was made that only the men could go. . . . I had just finished a tour of duty with the NAACP and had ridden a lot of Jim Crow buses and wanted very much to go, but I guess it was decided that I was too frail to make such a journey.

I think the period that is most important to most of us now is the period when we began to question whether we really wanted in. Even though the sit-in movement started off primarily as a method of getting in, it led to the concept of questioning whether it was worth trying to get in. The first effort was to be able to sit down at the lunch counters. When you look back and think of all the tragedy and suffering that the first sit-inners went through you begin to wonder, Why pay a price like that for the privilege of eating at lunch counters? There were those who saw from the beginning that the struggle was much bigger than getting a hamburger at a lunch counter. There were those who saw from the beginning that it was part of the struggle for full dignity as a human being. So out of that came two things that to me are very significant. First, there was the concept of the trained finding their identity with the masses. Another thing that came out of it at a later period was that of leadership training. As the young people moved out into the community and finally were able to be accepted, they began to discover indigenous leaders. . . .

Around 1965 there began to develop a great deal of questioning about what is the role of women in the struggle. Out of it came a concept that black women had to bolster the ego of the male. This implied that the black male had been treated in such a manner as to have been emasculated both by the white society and black women because the female was the head of the household. We began to deal with the question of the need of black women to play the subordinate role. I personally have never thought of this as being valid because it raises the question as to whether the black man is going to try to be a man on the basis of his capacity to deal with issues and situations rather than be a man because he has some people around him who claim him to be a man by taking subordinate roles.

I don't think you could go through the Freedom Movement without finding that the backbone of the support of the Movement were women. When demonstrations took place and when the community acted, usually it was some woman who came to the fore. . . .

I think at this stage the big question is, What is the American society? Is it the kind of society that either black women or black men or anyone who is seeing a dignified existence as a human being that permits people to grow and develop according to their capacity, that gives them a sense of value, not only for themselves, but a sense of value for other human beings. Is this the kind of society that is going to permit that? I think there is a great question as to whether it can become that kind of society. . . .

In order for us as poor and oppressed people to become a part of a society that is meaningful, the system under which we now exist has to be radically changed. This means that we are going to have to learn to think in *radical* terms. I use the term radical in its original meaning—getting down to and understanding the root cause. It means facing a system that does not lend itself to your needs and devising means by which you change that system. That is easier said than done. But one of the things that has to be faced is, in the process of wanting to change that system, how much have we got to do to find out who we are, where we have come from and where we are going. About twenty-eight years ago I used to go around making speeches, and I would open up my talk by saying that there was a man who had a health problem and he was finally told by the doctor that they could save his sight or save his memory, but they couldn't save both. They asked him which did he want and he said, "Save my sight because I would rather see where I am going than remember where I have been." I am saying as you must say, too, that in order to see where we are going, we not only must remember where we've been, but *we must understand where we have been*. This calls for a great deal of analytical thinking and evaluation of methods that have been used. We have to begin to think in terms of where do we really want to go and how can we get there.

Finally, I think it is also to be said that it is not a job that is going to be done by all the people simultaneously. Some will have to be in cadres, the advanced cadres, and some will have to come later. But one of the guiding principles has to be that we cannot lead a struggle that involves masses of people without getting the people to understand what their potentials are, what their strengths are.

12

Pauli Murray

1910–1985

A Renaissance person by any standard, Pauli Murray was brilliant and complex. She was a prolific writer; a civil and human rights activist; a brilliant lawyer, who graduated first in her class at Howard University and who was lauded by Thurgood Marshall for her strategic approach to civil rights litigation; a founder of the National Organization for Women and the Congress of Racial Equality (CORE); and the first African American to become an Episcopal priest. She also challenged gender identity, changing her name from Anna Pauline to Pauli.

12

Pauli Murray

1910–1985

The legal [illegible] [illegible]. She [illegible] and [illegible] rights act[illegible] [illegible] was [illegible] graduated first in her class at Howard University, and [illegible] was [illegible] Thurgood Marshall [illegible] strategy [illegible] [illegible] a founder of the National Organization for Women and the Congress of Racial Equality (CORE) and the [illegible] African American to become an Episcopal priest. She also [illegible] gender identity, changing her name from Anna Pauline to Pauli.

The Negro Woman in the Quest for Equality (Excerpts)

National Council of Negro Women, November 14, 1963, Washington, DC

Negro women, historically, have carried the dual burden of Jim Crow and Jane Crow. They have not always carried it graciously but they have carried it effectively. . . . In the course of their climb, Negro women have had to fight against the stereotypes of "female dominance" on the one hand and loose morals on the other hand, both growing out of the roles forced upon them during the slavery experience and its aftermath. But out of their struggle for human dignity, they also developed a tradition of independence and self-reliance. . . .

In the human rights battle, America has seen the image of the Negro evolving through many women. . . . Not only have women whose names are well known given this great human effort its peculiar vitality but women in the many communities whose names will never be known have revealed the courage and strength of the Negro woman. These are the mothers who have stood in school yards with their children, many times alone. These are the images which have touched America's heart. Painful as these experiences have been, one cannot help asking: would the Negro struggle have come this far without the indomitable determination of its women?

Recent disquieting events have made imperative an assessment of the role of the Negro woman in the quest for equality. The civil rights revolt, like many social upheavals, has released powerful pent-up emotions, cross currents, rivalries and hostilities. . . . There is much jockeying for position as ambitious men push and elbow that way to leadership roles. . . .

What emerges most clearly from events of the past several months is the tendency to assign women to a secondary, ornamental or "honoree" role instead of the partnership role in the civil rights movement which they have earned by their courage, intelligence, and dedication. It was bitterly humiliating for Negro women on August 28 to see themselves accorded little more than token recognition in the historic March on Washington. Not a single woman was invited to make one of the major speeches or to be part of the delegation of leaders who went to the White House. This omission was deliberate. Representations for recognition of women were made to the policy-making body sufficiently in advance of the August 28 arrangements to have permitted the necessary adjustments of the program. What the Negro women leaders were told is revealing: that no representation was given to them because they would not be able to agree on a delegate. How familiar was this excuse! It is a typical response from an entrenched power group. . . .

I have touched only briefly upon some of the important issues and problem areas which Negro women need to examine in their quest for equality. . . . How these issues are resolved may very well determine the outcome of the integration effort. One thing is crystal clear. The Negro woman can no longer postpone or subordinate the fight against discrimination because of sex to the civil rights struggle but must carry on both fights simultaneously. She must insist upon a partnership role in the integration movement. For, as

Mr. Justice William O. Douglas, speaking for the United States Supreme Court, has declared, "The two sexes are not fungible; a community made up exclusively of one is different from a community composed of both; the subtle interplay of influence of one on the other is among the imponderables." Clearly, therefore, the full participation and leadership of Negro women is necessary to the success of the civil rights revolution.

Moreover, Negro women should seek to communicate and cooperate with white women wherever possible. Their common problems and interests as women provide a bridge to span initial self-consciousness. Many white women today are earnestly seeking to make common cause with Negro women and are holding out their hands. All too often they find themselves rebuffed. Integration, however, is a two-way effort and Negro women must be courageous enough to grasp the hand whenever it is held out.

The path ahead will not be easy; the challenges to meet new standards of achievement in the search for equality will be many and bewildering. For a time, even, the casualties of integration may be great. But as Negro women in the United States enter their second century of emancipation from chattel slavery, let them be proud of their heritage and resolute in their determination to pass the best of it along to their children. As Lorraine Hansberry, the gifted playwright, has said, "For above all, in behalf of an ailing world which sorely needs our defiance, may we, as Negroes or women, never accept the notion of—'our place.'"

13

Dorothy I. Height

1912–2010

Dorothy Irene Height was one of the most legendary and influential Black women of her time. She advised Eleanor Roosevelt and presidents from Franklin Delano Roosevelt through Barack Obama. A disciple of another legend, Mary McLeod Bethune, of the National Council of Negro Women (NCNW), Height later became the organization's president and served in that position for four decades. She was the only woman of what was called the Big Six of civil rights leaders and she was instrumental in organizing the 1963 March on Washington. Her visionary work in Africa aided freedom struggles on that continent and she was active in the anti-apartheid movement for South Africa. Height was instrumental in efforts to support and lift up the Black family with the NCNW's Black Family Reunion. She also chaired the Leadership Conference on Civil Rights.

Untitled Speech at the Opening of the Bethune Museum and Archives for Black Women

November 13, 1979, Washington, DC

Height gave the following speech at a symposium on the legacy of the NCNW. The conference marked the opening of the Bethune Museum and Archives for Black Women in Washington, DC, the first institution devoted exclusively to Black women's history.

I came into office at a time when we were struggling very hard as black women in this country, seeking to get hold of our organization and to hold our heads high in the society around us. One of the things that had confronted us was that we were the inheritors of a great organization headed by Mrs. Bethune, and we did not have tax-exempt status. And, I think there are people in this room who remember as I do, how we stood on the floor and said, "If it means we have to give up political action, let's not worry about it." And we struggled on. We could not get any contributions based upon the person's being exempt.

So, one of the first things that we did was to seek a way to give us the chance to expand our program so that the political activity that we can never give up would not—would somehow be in balance with the rest of it. And I think the educational foundation that was established—and Daisy Lampkin served as its chair and Dorothy Ferebee followed her—was a means through which we were able to initiate some kind—new kinds of program activities. And one of the first of these was the Bethune House here in Washington, the first 221-D.C. housing program sponsored by a non-governmental organization.

But it was very shortly thereafter that the country was caught up in something else. It was moving towards what we had said in the NAACP, we would be "free by '63." But little did we know the events that would somehow step up around us. [*Previous speaker*] Mrs. Mason has referred to Rosa Parks and you know the story of Montgomery. And you know what that did to the whole nation and what it set in motion; the sit-ins, the pray-ins, all the different kind of things that were happening. And in the middle of all of that as the things began to move, the Taconic Foundation, under the leadership of Stephen Currier, wanted to know what could be done to help deal with the problems of the black community, and the black family. And they called together Roy Wilkins and Whitney Young, and Martin Luther King Jr., James Farmer, C. Eric Lincoln—who had written a book on the black Muslims—A. Phillip Randolph, Jack Greenberg—who was with the NAACP Legal Defense Fund—and me. And made us pledge that we would somehow stay together, never send a substitute but come ourselves to each meeting, and that we would dedicate one day every six weeks to thinking together about where we were.

And I remember that each one took an assignment. I took the assignment of organizations because I was interested in organizations. And one of the significant things that I think we often forget is that black people and black women have been as shut out of volunteer opportunities on boards and committees and organizations outside of their own [communities]—they've been just as shut out there as we are out of jobs. And so I began to work with that kind of study. And someone else took housing and away we went. And then suddenly something happened: Medgar Evers was assassinated. And, on the morning after his assassination, Stephen Currier called us all back together again and he said, "We've been thinking of ourselves as a kind of united civil rights leadership." But he said, "What we need to do now is to see how this country can be brought to a realization, that it cannot exist with this kind of thing happening, and what all this signifies."

He sent out telegrams to a hundred people to meet at the Carlisle Hotel the next morning. Ninety-some persons appeared, and he had each of us tell the story of the organization and its driving. Roy Wilkins had to leave for the funeral of Medgar Evers. And, then after that, the rest of us all had a chance to talk. I had to say what it meant to black women that we were a part of the whole civil rights movement, that we were a civil rights organization, really, under the leadership of women. And that we had had a major hand in that whole beginning with the significant male leadership, to point out that we had to add to that great group that started, the Student Non-violent Coordinating Committee, no matter what it was doing or who agreed with its tactics or not. Because as women, we could not see our children and our youth struggling and have them on the outside of our effort.

And after we had each told the stories, Stephen Currier made an appeal. He received pledges of some $800,000 for the civil rights movement. Those organizations that were tax-exempt could reap the full benefits. We were not tax-exempt, but we did have the educational arm, which was the educational foundation. So that as contributions were made, we received $50,000 from that civil rights pot. And I think I have to add there that another piece of money that came to us through the civil rights effort was from Martin Luther King Jr., who when he received the Nobel Peace Prize, came back and he said to all of us around the table, "I have to give every organization its piece." I think we know a lot about Dr. King, but I think that's a little known story of how he shared with each of those organizations.

From that little spark, we were asked also to perform another function, because we did have an educational foundation. We were asked to become the trustees for the funds the NAACP—which was not tax-exempt—gathered for the Evers children. And I'll always remember how Mrs. Lampkin, when the time came, said to us, "It is good that we did this because those were lean days at many points." But we held that money and the interest and it all went to that family and those children, because it was what people who had expressed their concern wanted them to have.

So that in a sense, the civil rights movement and our role in it shaped the task of anyone carrying leadership in the organization. It meant—and I look over here and I see Arnetta Wallace—that on a certain day after the four little girls were murdered in Birmingham, that we descended into Birmingham, 14 heads of national women's organizations, members of the National Council of Negro Women. And we were there, we marched through the bayonets and we felt the tension in the city.

Dr. Ferebee and I were there in Selma long before the Selma march. We went down at the time that Prathia Wynn and James Forman called us and said, "Three hundred children are in jail here and nobody knows where they are. We need some outside voice that will come in and help us to get that story out." And we got there just as the 300 children were released from jail, and some of their pictures looked like the children in Cambodia because they were bare bones; they had been denied food and services. And when we asked them, "What have you been having?" one little boy said, "We've been eating boll weevil gravy." And when I looked at some of the children and I said to them, "You say so many bad things about people here. Don't you think there are some good white people?" And the little boy who had said the most looked up and he said—he looked at Dr. Ferebee and me—and he said, "Well, there must be some." [laughter] But you know, it was a driving thing to think that you live in a country where a child of one race would say, "There must be somebody of the other race who's decent."

And all of that kept pushing us. We went to Atlanta and brought together representatives—young women—who had been the victims of law enforcement officers in the jails. We heard them tell about the vaginal searches by orderlies who dipped their gloves in Lysol. We heard them tell about how they banned together, so that they would not be raped by the officers all around them. And we found ourselves, little by little, pulling together all our forces to say, "What is there we can do?" And I remember the meeting that we had in Atlanta, when we were talking about this, because we brought together white women's groups also, that they might know what was happening, as well.

And I'll never forget; we called it the Women's Interorganizational Committee, because we didn't know what to call it. We didn't want to say it was a civil rights meeting. And when the meeting was over, one of the women said, "Well, you know, the initials of what we call [ourselves] is WIC. And it if means that if each one of us, no matter whether we are black or white, should go back into her community and be like a wick, lighted, that could be—that little bit of light, that could make a difference. And, out of that, the whole concept of WICS was developed.

And when we were called upon to reach young women in poverty, the very coalition we had put together became the one that Sargent Shriver could call upon to help recruit young women for the Job Corps. And someone said, "What shall we call it?" And I remember Helen Racklin saying, "Well we already have WIC," so we called it Women in Community Service.

In other words, the National Council of Negro Women has been there even when our story has not been told. You may remember that in the summer of 1963, there was a great march on Washington. We were there. We did something that we were asked not to do, but it was too late when we heard they were asking that no one meet after the march on Washington. We held a meeting called "After the March, What?" And out of that meeting, there came a molding of some new spirits and new interests. So that by 1964, when Bob Moses called for the summer in Mississippi, the freedom schools, we had a coalition of women already working together, and those women went down into Mississippi on Wednesdays. Etta Barnett is one of them, who is here tonight.

And we went in interracial teams with an idea that was designed by Polly Cowan, that we would go in to see what was happening to young people in the freedom schools. But that we would always carry our talents and we would always do something that would be significant. So out of Wednesdays in Mississippi, we began to build bridges of understanding between black and white women in the South and black and white women in communities across the country. And one of the significant things that had happened in that Atlanta meeting I mentioned was that we asked the women who were there, because so much was being said about, you know, "Yankees stay home; don't interfere with what's going on in the South." We asked them a question: "Does it help you or does it hinder you to have a national organization come in?" And, the women, Clarice Harvey, speaking for one group of women said, "We're from Jackson, Miss. We are black and white women. We are seeing each other here and knowing each other for the first time. But we know one thing, we will never be apart again." And then she said, "Don't give up. A national organization is like a long-handled spoon: you can come in and stir us up and get us moving."

I always thought that that was a good demonstration of what Mrs. Bethune had in mind, in saying that when you think about it, there is no such thing as just being local when you're part of a national movement. And that sense of being a part of a national movement came through in some very real ways. We had after that, workshops in Mississippi, which got us into housing—into housing with low-income families. We were working with hunger, pig banks—we established pig banks and pig agreements with families. Because the people we saw in the workshops in Mississippi said to us, "We are concerned about our rights, but we have no jobs and our children have to eat." And so we helped them to see how to plant gardens, how to—I don't know, you don't grow pigs—[laughter] raise pigs, I guess; how to deal with pigs and we taught them how to feed them. And some of those people said to us afterwards, "We learned through those pigs that it makes a difference what you eat. And many of us have never had the food that we needed."

Today, the National Council of Negro Women is able to report that we have assets that are some four to five million dollars. But we could not have even thought about this before 1965 when we got our tax exemption. December 1, 1965. There's a recent report just released on philanthropy to women's organizations. And it cites five organizations and we rank third in terms of organizations who have received substantial support from foundations. In 1966, when the Ford Foundation made us a grant of $300,000, that was the most that it or any other foundation had given to a women's organization. 1966. Just think of that. So it shows you where women's groups were.

Out of that experience, we learned one thing: that the Council, in order to do the job, had to have the supporting services of staff. We had to have staff who could understand that they were part of an organization that is essentially volunteer, but that their job was to be a part of a partnership and to be supportive. And so today across this country, in some 20 locations, we have moved to the point where we have staff working at many different levels. There are some 146 of them. There are 72 who will be in this convention. But the important thing is not their numbers, nor that there are jobs, but it is the realization that where black women are in a society requires that we have the capability to work at our needs not after hours but all through the day. That some of that continuity has to come through the kind of devoted, skilled work that staff give: disciplined and directed, but responsive to the interests and concerns of the volunteers and the membership of the National Council of Negro Women.

I think another piece of movement I'd like to mention that I think has affected us over these years, came because we were working to put [a statue of] Mrs. Bethune in Lincoln Park. When we started out in 1960, people said this was, you know, just something that we were discussing. But how could we stand to see Abraham Lincoln with a slave at his knee, put there by the emancipated group in 1874 with the funds raised by the newly emancipated citizens, and not try to place on the other end of that park a memorial that would say black people have made a contribution in American life? Charlotte Scott gave the first five dollars she earned in her freedom to start the Emancipation Group. And, so we called upon people across the country to respond.

In the course of things Abraham Lincoln was turned around so that his back would not face Mrs. Bethune. [*laughter*] Every time we say that, the Interior Department corrects us and says, "He was not turned around; he was repositioned." [*laughter and applause*]

Another movement that hit us very hard was the movement of women. And when you ask me the question that you've asked us all about [which was worse], racism or sexism, I have to say that the

International Women's Year found itself with a unique contribution because, not only of our domestic work, but of our international interests and the things that we have tried to do. Because it was at that time, at the 100th anniversary of Mrs. Bethune's birth, that we were determined that we would make and expand on the international interests. There's so many things. Mrs. Mason and I were in Haiti working in the name of the National Council of Negro Women to get the vote for women there. I thought for the moment it was Mrs. Bethune's administration and I asked Vivian today and she said no, it was Dr. Ferebee's administration. But they all used the same techniques. I was then president of Delta Sigma Theta, and we were called and asked to go. Vivian represented the Council; Laura Lovely, [*inaudible*] Kappa Alpha, and I, Delta Sigma Theta, and when we said, "Where are the funds?" They said, "Oh, well of course we know your groups will see that you get there." [*laughter*] And they did, but that's the way the Council was represented for years and years. For we went into our pockets and when you got there you said, "I represent the National Council of Negro Women." [*laughter and applause*] And, you were proud to do it!

So it was to be understood that in International Women's Year, we would get support to have at Mexico City, a group of women from Africa and from the Caribbean. And then we had the chance to bring them back with us to let them see the pig banks; to go to visit the housing; to visit people; and then to join us for the 100th birthday celebration of Mary McLeod Bethune at Bethune-Cookman College. And, I tell you, that is an occasion that we will never forget.

But it also heightened the fact that we are part of a whole women's movement. I think very strongly that no group has more right to say that than we. Bill Trent tells a story that's a favorite of mine. He says that Mrs. Bethune once had a meeting in Memphis, and she'd asked a nationally known black male to make the keynote address. And as he stood, he looked at the women and he said, "If you women would be as concerned about what you put in your heads, as what you are about what you have on heads, our race would be better off." And, he said at that point, Mrs. Bethune rose and said, "Thank you sir, you have said quite enough." [*laughter and applause*] "The women will decide what they have on their heads and what they put in their heads." [*laughter and applause*]

Now, I think any organization that follows that has to be concerned about women. But when you ask me the question about race and sex, I want to add something else that I saw recently in a poster. And that poster was a woman who had two chains; she was chained down with two very heavy pieces of stone, with chains on her legs. And the heading underneath was "Double Trouble." And the idea that it reflected was, take one away—one said "racism" and the other said "sexism"—take one away and she is still tied down. Take the other away and leave that one, she's still tied down. The only way she will make it: they both have to be eliminated. [*applause*] And I think that as we move into our convention with an idea of imperatives for the '80s, we need to work very hard to eliminate both racism and sexism.

Two things I want to say about our internal life. One is that the spirit of collaboration and cooperation that has been expressed in the wider society has also touched us. In 1969, we had a meeting at Nassau, in which the national organizations comprising the National Council of Negro Women said, "It is so important to build this power that we must get every member we can in our organizations to become a direct member. And that small amount that each one contributes each year, can help us to build our strength." We're far from achieving that goal, but seven of our national organizations, even this year, have called upon their members to do this and it is coming in steadily. Because you know, as I think it was Billie

Holiday [who] said it, "Mama may have and Papa may have, but God bless the child that's got his own." [*applause*]

Now, because as proud as we are of what we have achieved, the fact is that today we have about a 99 percent batting average in our request for government and foundation support. But we are concerned that we also keep building that internal support, because those funds come but they're earmarked, you're not free to use them. It is what we do ourselves that makes the difference. Now the other thing that is a characteristic we've been working on, is the realization that with revenue sharing, with the new federalism, with everything moving to the states, black women had better learn to get themselves together in those states, because [*applause*] decisions are being made in the states. And while we considered clustering areas and regions, we now are trying to see that we look at the status as the black women in each of the states and try to amass our power there.

So, you see, we are in the state of still becoming. We have so far to go. But I remember two things that were said this morning, that have kind of stayed with me all day. It was what Jeanetta Welch Brown said when she said, [there's been] a lot of talk about some of the early days—and each of us could tell you a whole lot of things—but what she said came through to me: "There's been a lot of suffering that has gone into building the National Council of Negro Women." A lot of people in many places have put a lot into it. And then Sue Bailey Thurman, remember what she said in her message: "This is an organization of women with caring hearts." I look back and realize that I've been a part of the Council since 1937. And I don't think that outside of my mother and my church, there's been anything, any person of greater influence than Mary McLeod Bethune. And I think the thing that I'm sure if we could all say it as a trio, we would want to say, is that the thing about the

National Council of Negro Women that is its greatest source of strength, is the depth of the vision of the dream that Mrs. Bethune left with us.

Who, except a great dreamer could be born of slave parents, could struggle in the fields of South Carolina, and leave a legacy that begins with the words, "I leave you love"? And if you take this message, it seems to me, that when we look to what's to happen in the future, it isn't going to be just by, you know, designating this post, or that post, or this staff or that volunteer, or this whatever. It's going to be the extent to which all of us rededicate ourselves—whether we are members of Council or not—to the idea of seeing how caring hearts take hold of a mission and keep it relevant, because what we did in '79 is not going to be good enough in the '80s. Thank you.

14
Margaret Walker Alexander
1915–1998

A poet and a novelist, Margaret Walker Alexander became immersed in Black history and literature at a very early age. Her writings explored and promoted the Black experience, with emphasis on the liberation of Black women. She was the first Black woman to be honored with the Yale Series of Younger Poets Award for her first poetry collection, *For My People* (1942). She published the novel *Jubilee* in 1966.

Discovering Our Connections: Race, Gender, and the Law

Keynote address, Discovering Our Connections: Race and Gender in Theory and Practice of the Law Symposium, hosted by the *American University Journal of Gender, Social Policy and the Law,* Washington College of Law, September 12, 1992, Washington, DC

The great American poet, Walt Whitman wrote:

I feel I am of them—
I belong to those convicts and prostitutes myself—
And henceforth I will not deny them—
For how can I deny myself?

In these United States of America justice is tempered by money and power. Ever since the Constitution was framed more than two hundred years ago the power structure of America has been composed largely of white Anglo-Saxon Protestant males—no Catholics, Jews, nor Negroes need apply. These excluded groups along with all women were considered the minorities. When the society is fascist, sexist, and racist, the judicial system can be neither better nor worse. But the law is of a dual nature. It is both an oppressor and a liberator. When segregation was the law of the land established in 1896 by the Supreme Court in the Plessy-Ferguson case, the law was an oppressor.

Even before the Civil War under the Black Codes or penal system Black males were counted three-fifths of human beings and women were not counted as either citizens or human beings. After a brief period of twenty-five to thirty years when Black males under radical reconstruction obtained the vote and held political office, Plessy-Ferguson revoked this privilege and disenfranchised most Black males. In 1919, after a fifty-four years struggle, white women received the franchise, but Black women were still for the most part without the franchise until as late as 1965 when the Voting Rights Act made voting for all citizens a universal act—all races and genders included.

Racism, Classism, and Sexism are pernicious evils and these three evils still persist in corrupting American society. Black people in this country have historically been the poorest of the poor masses. Money and power persist in excluding most African Americans. The Thirteenth Amendment which was designed to eliminate slavery added a clause which excluded criminals from emancipation. It reads, "except in the case of criminal actions." Thus, it is no wonder that the disproportionate numbers of Black males or African-Americans are in our overcrowded jails and, therefore, without voting rights.

The judicial system remains today both a liberating and oppressive force where RACE and GENDER are concerned. Whether in the realm of constitutional, civil, or criminal law, our American judicial system discriminates against most minorities including women.

In Antebellum days the records show that Black women were beaten, branded, and murdered with no recourse to the law which frequently included the over-seer as sheriff and the master as judge and prosecuting lawyer. As late as the nineteen sixties, a Black woman, Fannie Lou Hamer, was beaten in a Winona, Mississippi jail by two Black trusties until she could not move. Sterling

Brown used to tell a folk tale about American justice where a goose was taken into custody by a fox and when she went to court the judge, jury, jailer, and prosecuting attorney were all foxes. African-Americans are well aware that when the goose is Black all the foxes may be white—judge, jury, and executioner. In 1952, Judge William Hastie spoke at Jackson State University at a seminar on American democracy and a white man asked him if he thought the law could legislate men's minds and hearts and thus, end segregation. Judge Hastie answered, "We are going to make segregation illegal in this country and then we'll go from there."

During the past fifty years I have encountered the American judicial system at least on four different occasions. I hasten to add I have never been arrested nor spent the night in jail. I learned, however, during the 1960s that it is not always a disgrace to do so. A famous quote from Civil Disobedience by Henry David Thoreau says, "In an unjust state the only place for a just man is in jail."

In the early 1940s, in New York City, when my husband was flat on his back in an Army hospital in Wales, I was summoned to court on a charge of breaking and entering. I secured a good lawyer who later became a judge in New York City—and taking my infant daughter—I went to court. I lost the case and I was evicted from a coldwater flat in Greenwich Village where no Negroes had ever been allowed.

In the early 1970s, my son who volunteered for service in the Marines returned from a tour of duty in Vietnam. Two months after he returned he was arrested in a Black Nationalist Group of eleven persons including two women, one who was pregnant. They were accused and indicted for the murder of a white policeman. After seven weeks and a habeas corpus hearing, he was released on his own recognizance together with most of his friends. This was an example of false arrest. The incident succeeded in preventing my accepting a Fulbright grant to teach in Trondheim, Norway.

In 1970, two days before two students were killed at Jackson State University by highway patrolmen, L. Patrick Gray came to visit me in my home. He was accompanied by a man from the FBI who refused to identify himself. When the killings occurred, Mr. Gray telephoned me to ask what I thought caused the incident. I told him violent white racism and the widening of the Indo-China war in Cambodia were the causes of campus unrest and if they do not stop the war we will lose our country. Subsequently, when the President's Commission on Campus Unrest held a hearing in Jackson, I was called as a witness and asked to testify. I repeated what I told L. Patrick Gray.

During the same decade, nearly thirty years after my first experience with the judicial system in New York City, I had a mixed decision—I sued the apparent author of a block buster book for copyright infringement of my novel, *Jubilee.* The judge ordered a hearing by a female magistrate. She rendered the decision in my favor returning the case to the district judge. He ignored the female magistrate's opinion. Instead, he wrote a strong opinion against me and within ten days, retired or resigned his judgeship.

Four years ago in 1988, my biography of Richard Wright was published by Warner Books. Six months later, his widow, Mrs. Ellen Wright, sued for copyright infringement. Eighteen months later, we won the decision. Then she appealed and the Appellate Court upheld the District Court's decision.

My experiences certainly did not endear me to the system—particularly having to give a deposition. But after nearly a year since the last skirmish which happily we won I still believe what I said in the beginning: Money and power temper justice in our judicial system. People always ask, "What is it you people want? Haven't you made progress? What kind of change do you want?" We want a judicial system that treats all people alike, regardless of race, class, and gender—where the law is more the liberator than the oppressor where women have more than voting rights, but also have reproductive rights—thus, having some control over our bodies and our destinies!

Recently, a reporter from *Mother Jones* magazine came to see me and asked how I could live in Mississippi with all the police brutality there. I wrote an answer to him in the form of a poem and here it is—

On Police Brutality:

I remember Memorial Day Massacre
Nineteen thirty-seven in Chicago.
And I was in the Capital of D.C.
May of nineteen seventy-one
When they beat all those white heads
And put two thousand souls in jail.
I wasn't in South Commons Boston
Neither when Crispus Attucks died
Nor South Boston when the rednecks rioted.
But I remember Boston
Where I couldn't buy a hot pastrami sandwich
In a greasy joint.
I remember living there in fear,
Much as some would feel in Mississippi
I was neither in Watts, Los Angeles, California
In nineteen sixty-five
Nor Detroit in nineteen sixty-seven
And I remember all the fuss over LeRoi Jones
In Newark, New Jersey, too.
Now Santa Barbara, California is remembered
As a separate incident, a separate thing
From Kent State in Ohio And Jackson State in Mississippi

And Orangeburg, South Carolina
And Texas Southern
But to me, they were all of one piece
Of the same old racist rag.
And all of these things are part
Of what I call Police Brutality.

For My People

November 1939

For my people everywhere singing their slave songs
repeatedly: their dirges and their ditties and their blues
and jubilees, praying their prayers nightly to an
unknown god, bending their knees humbly to an
unseen power;
For my people lending their strength to the years, to the
gone years and the now years and the maybe years,
washing ironing cooking scrubbing sewing mending
hoeing plowing digging planting pruning patching
dragging along never gaining never reaping never
knowing and never understanding;
For my playmates in the clay and dust and sand of Alabama
backyards playing baptizing and preaching and doctor
and jail and soldier and school and mama and cooking
and playhouse and concert and store and hair and
Miss Choomby and company;
For the cramped bewildered years we went to school to learn

to know the reasons why and the answers to and the
people who and the places where and the days when, in
memory of the bitter hours when we discovered we
were black and poor and small and different and nobody
cared and nobody wondered and nobody understood;
For the boys and girls who grew in spite of these things to
be man and woman, to laugh and dance and sing and
play and drink their wine and religion and success, to
marry their playmates and bear children and then die
of consumption and anemia and lynching;
For my people thronging 47th Street in Chicago and Lenox
Avenue in New York and Rampart Street in New
Orleans, lost disinherited dispossessed and happy
people filling the cabarets and taverns and other
people's pockets and needing bread and shoes and milk and
land and money and something—something all our own;
For my people walking blindly spreading joy, losing time
being lazy, sleeping when hungry, shouting when
burdened, drinking when hopeless, tied, and shackled
and tangled among ourselves by the unseen creatures
who tower over us omnisciently and laugh;
For my people blundering and groping and floundering in
the dark of churches and schools and clubs
and societies, associations and councils and committees and
conventions, distressed and disturbed and deceived and
devoured by money-hungry glory-craving leeches,
preyed on by facile force of state and fad and novelty, by
false prophet and holy believer;
For my people standing staring trying to fashion a better way
from confusion, from hypocrisy and misunderstanding,
trying to fashion a world that will hold all the people,

all the faces, all the adams and eves and their countless generations;

Let a new earth rise. Let another world be born. Let a
bloody peace be written in the sky. Let a second
generation full of courage issue forth; let a people
loving freedom come to growth. Let a beauty full of
healing and a strength of final clenching be the pulsing
in our spirits and our blood. Let the martial songs
be written, let the dirges disappear. Let a race of men now
rise and take control.

15

Gwendolyn Brooks

1917–2000

Gwendolyn Brooks was the first Black author to win the Pulitzer Prize for Poetry (1949), for her volume of poems *Annie Allen*. She was also poet laureate of Illinois and poetry consultant to the Library of Congress. Her writing was always meticulous, creative, and purposeful. She was dedicated to reaching new audiences and to inspiring young Black writers—which she did over a long and productive career.

Speech to the Young: Speech to the Progress-Toward (Among Them Nora and Henry III)

Say to them,
say to the down-keepers,
the sun-slappers,
the self-soilers,
the harmony-hushers,
"Even if you are not ready for day
it cannot always be night."
You will be right.
For that is the hard home-run.

Live not for battles won.
Live not for the-end-of-the-song.
Live in the along.

16

Fannie Lou Hamer

1917–1977

A person of heroic courage and integrity, Fannie Lou Hamer spent much of her life as a sharecropper in rural Mississippi before leaping headfirst into the long struggle for equal voting rights. Hamer lost her job and endured beatings and threats on her life as an organizer for the Student Nonviolent Coordinating Committee (SNCC) and the Mississippi Freedom Democratic Party. She was a passionate and compelling speaker whose appearance at the 1964 Democratic National Convention, where she took America to task for its racism, riveted the nation.

I'm Sick and Tired of Being Sick and Tired

December 20, 1964, Harlem, New York

Hamer delivered this speech with Malcolm X at a rally at the Williams Institutional CME Church, Harlem, New York, that was organized to support the Mississippi Freedom Democratic Party's Congressional Challenge.

My name is Fannie Lou Hamer and I exist at 626 East Lafayette Street in Ruleville, Mississippi. The reason I say "exist" [is] because we're excluded from everything in Mississippi but the tombs and the graves. That's why it is called that instead of the "land of the free and the home of the brave." It's called in Mississippi "the land of the tree and the home of the grave."

It was the 31st of August of 1962, that eighteen of us traveled 26 miles to the county courthouse in Indianola, Mississippi, to try to register to become first-class citizens. It was the 31st of August in 1962, that I was fired for trying to become a first-class citizen.

When we got to Indianola on the 31st of August in 1962, we was met there by the state highway patrolmen, the city policemen and anybody—as some of you know that have worked in Mississippi, any white man that is able to wear a khaki pair of pants without them falling off him and holding two guns can make a good law officer—so we was met by them there.

After taking this literacy test, some of you have seen it, we have 21 questions and some is not questions. It began with: "Write the date of this application. What is your full name. By whom are you employed"—so we can be fired by the time we get back home—"Are you a citizen of the United States and an inhabitant of Mississippi. Have you ever been convicted of any of the following crimes."—when, if the people would be convicted of the following crimes, the registrar wouldn't be there. But after we go through this process of filling out this literacy form, we are asked to copy a section of the constitution of Mississippi and after we've copied this section of the constitution of Mississippi we are asked to give a reasonable interpretation to tell what it meant, what we just copied that we just seen for the first time.

After finishing this form, we started on this trip back to Ruleville, Mississippi, and we was stopped by the same city policeman that I had seen in Indianola and a state highway patrolman. We was ordered to get off the bus. After we got off the bus, we was ordered to get back on the bus and told to go back to Indianola. When we got back to Indianola the bus driver was charged with driving a bus the wrong color. That's very true. This same bus had been used year after year to haul people to the cotton fields to pick cotton and to chop cotton. But, this day, for the first time that this bus had been used for voter registration it had the wrong color. They first charged this man one hundred dollars. And from a hundred dollars they cut down to fifty. And from fifty to thirty, and after they got down to thirty dollars the eighteen of us had enough among ourselves to pay his fine.

Then we continued this journey back to Ruleville. When we got to Ruleville, Reverend Jeff Sunny drove me out to this rural area where I had been existing for the past eighteen years as a timekeeper and a sharecropper. I was met there by my daughter and my husband's cousin that told me this man was raising a lot of Cain because I had went to Indianola. My oldest girl said that she believed I would have to leave there. Then my husband came and during the time he was talking this white man walked up and asked him had I made it back: And he told him I had. And he said, "Well, did you tell her what I said!" My husband told him he did and I walked out. He said, "Fannie Lou," he say, "did Pap tell you what I said!" And I told him he did. He said, "I mean that. You will have to go down and withdraw or you will have to leave."

I said, "Mr. Marlow," I said, "I wasn't trying to register for you today. I was trying to register for myself." And this was it. I had to leave that same night.

On the tenth of September in 1962, sixteen bullets were fired into the home of Mr. and Mrs. Robert Tucker, where I'd been living after I was fired from this plantation. That same night, two girls was shot in Ruleville. They also shot in Mr. Joe McDonald's home that same night. And until this day the place was swamped with FBI, until this day—it's a very small town where everybody knows everybody—it hadn't been one arrest made.

That's why about four months ago when the FBI came to talk to me about my life being threatened—they wanted to know what could I tell them about it—I told them until they straightened out some of the things that we had done happened, don't come asking about the things that just happened. Do something about the problems that we'd already had. And I made it plain. I said, "If there is a God and a heaven." I said, "if I was going to see you two up there, I would tell them to send me back to Mississippi because I know He wouldn't be just to let you up there." This probably don't sound too good to everybody, but if I can't tell the truth—just tell me to sit down—because I have to tell it like it is.

The 3rd day of June, we went to a voter educational workshop and was returning back to Mississippi. We arrived in Winona, Mississippi, between ten-thirty and eleven o'clock on the 9th of June. Some of the people got off the bus to go in the restaurant and two of the people got off the bus to use the washroom. I was still on the Continental Trailways bus and looking through the window, I saw the people rush out of the restaurant and then the two people rush out had got off to use the washroom. One of the people that had got off to use the washroom got on the bus and I got off the bus. I went straight to Miss [Annell] Ponder, it was five of them had got off the bus, six in all but one had got back on the bus, so that was five. I went to talk to Miss Ponder to ask of her what had happened. And she said that it was state highway patrolmen and a city chief of police had tapped them all on the shoulder with billy clubs and ordered them out. And I said, "Well, this is Mississippi."

I went back and got on the bus. When I looked back through the window they was putting those people in the patrolmen's car. I got off of the bus, holding the eyes of Miss Ponder and she screamed to tell me to get back on the bus when somebody screamed from her car and said, "Get that one, too." And a man jumped out of his car and said, "You are under arrest." As he went to open the door, he opened the door and told me to get in. And as I started to get in, he kicked me and I was carried to the county jailhouse by this county deputy and a plainclothesman. They would call me all kinds of names. They would ask me questions and when I would attempt to answer the questions, they would curse and tell me to hush.

I was carried to the county jail and when I got inside of the jail, they had the other five already in the booking room. When I walked in the booking room, one of the city policemen just walked over, a very tall man, walked over and jumped on one of the young men's feet, James West from Itta Bena, Mississippi. Then they began to place us in cells. They left some of the people out of the cell and I was placed in a cell with Miss Euvester Simpson from Itta Bena.

After they left the people in the booking room I began to hear the sounds of licks and I began to hear screams. I couldn't see the people, but I could hear them. And I would hear somebody when they would say, "Can't you say 'yes, sir,' nigger? Can't you say 'yes, sir'?" And they would call Annell Ponder awful names.

And she would say, "Yes, I can say 'yes, sir." And they would tell her, "Well, say it."

She said, "I don't know you well enough."

And I would hear when she would hit the floor again. I don't know how long this happened until after awhile I saw Miss Ponder pass my cell. And her clothes had been ripped off from the shoulder down to the waist. Her hair was standing up on her head. Her mouth was swollen and bleeding. And one of her eyes looked like blood. And they put her in a cell where I couldn't see her.

And then three men came to my cell. The state highway patrolman asked me where I was from. And I told him I was from Ruleville. He said, "We're going to check that." And they left the cell and after awhile they came back. And he told me, said, "You were right." he said. "You's from Ruleville all right and we going to make you wish you was dead." I was led out of that cell and into another cell where they had two Negro prisoners. The state highway patrolman gave the first Negro prisoner the blackjack. It was a long heavy leather something made with something you could hold it, and it was loaded with either rocks or something metal. And they ordered me to lie down on the bed on my face. And I was beat by that first Negro until he was exhausted. I was beat until he was ordered by the state highway patrolman to stop.

After he told the first Negro to stop, he gave the blackjack to the second Negro. When the second Negro began to beat, it seemed like it was more than I could bear. I began to work my feet, and the state highway patrolman ordered the first Negro that had beat me to set on my feet where I was kicking them. My dress worked up real high and I smoothed my clothes down. And one of the city policemens walked over and pulled my dress as high as he could. I was trying to shield as many licks from my left side as I could because I had polio when I was six or eight years old. But when they had finished beating me, they were, while they was beating, I was screaming. One of the white men got up and began to beat me in my head.

A couple of Saturdays ago, I went to a doctor in Washington, D.C., a specialist, and he said one of the arteries behind this left eye had a blood clot. After this happened in jail, we was in jail from Monday until Wednesday without seeing a doctor. They had our trial on Tuesday and we was charged with disorderly conduct and resisting arrest. I was in jail when Medgar Evers was killed.

What I'm trying to point out now is when you take a very close look at this American society, it's time to question these things. We have made an appeal for the president of the United States and the attorney general to please protect us in Mississippi. And I can't understand how it's out of their power to protect people in Mississippi. They can't do that, but when a white man is killed in the Congo, they send people there.

And you can always hear this long sob story: "You know it takes time." For three hundred years, we've given them time. And I've been tired so long, now I am sick and tired of being sick and tired, and we want a change. We want a change in this society in America because, you see, we can no longer ignore the facts and getting our children to sing, "Oh say can you see, by the dawn's early light, what so proudly we hailed." What do we have to hail here? The truth is the only thing going to free us. And you know this whole society is sick. And to prove just how sick it was when we was in Atlantic City challenging the National Convention, when I was testifying before the Credentials Committee, I was cut off because they hate to see what they been knowing all the time and that's the truth.

Yes, a lot of people will roll their eyes at me today but I'm going to tell you just like it is, you see, it's time—you see, this is what got all this like this, there's so much hypocrisy in this society and if we want America to be a free society we have to stop telling lies, that's all. Because we're not free and you know we're not free. You're not free here in Harlem. I've gone to a lot of big cities and I've got my first city to go to where this man wasn't standing with his feet on this black man's neck.

And it's time for you to wake up because, you see, a lot of people say, "Oh, they is afraid of integration." But the white man is not afraid of integration, not with his kids. He's afraid of his wife's kids because he's got them all over the place. Because some of his kids just might be my second cousin.

And the reason we're here today, we're asking for support if this Constitution is really going to be of any help in this American society, the 4th day of January is when we'll find it out. This challenge that we're challenging the five representatives from Mississippi; now how can a man be in Washington, elected by the people, when 95 percent of the people cannot vote in Mississippi? Just taking a chance on trying to register to vote, you can be fired. Not only fired, you can be killed. You know it's true because you know what happened to Schwerner, Goodman, and Chaney. And any person that's working down there to change the system can be counted just as another nigger.

But some of the things I've got to say today may be a little sickening. People have said year after year, "Those people in Mississippi can't think." But after we would work ten and eleven hours a day for three lousy dollars and couldn't sleep we couldn't do anything else but think. And we have been thinking a long time. And we are tired of what's going on. And we want to see now, what this here will turn out for the 4th of January. We want to see is democracy real?

We want to see this because the challenge is based upon the violation of the Thirteenth, Fourteenth, and Fifteenth Amendments to the United States Constitution, which hadn't done anything for us yet. And the U.S. courts tied it to Section 201 and 226. Those people were illegally elected and they have been there—the man that I challenged, Jamie L. Whitten, has been in Washington thirteen years and he is not representing the people of Mississippi because not only do they discriminate against the poor Negroes, they discriminated up until the 3rd of November against the poor whites, but they let them vote because they wanted their votes. But it will run until the 1st of July and we need your support—morally, politically, and financially, too. We need your help.

And, people, you don't know in Harlem the power that you got. But you just don't try to use it. People never would have thought—the folks they said was just ignorant, common people out of Mississippi that would have tried to challenge the representatives from Mississippi. But you see the point is: we have been dying in Mississippi year after year for nothing. And I don't know, I may be bumped off as soon as I go back to Mississippi but what we should realize, people have been bumped off for nothing.

It is my goal for the cause of giving those Negro children a decent education in the state of Mississippi and giving them something that they have never had. Then I know my life won't be in vain. Because, not only do we need a change in the state of Mississippi, but we need a change here in Harlem. And it's time for every American citizen to wake up because now the whole world is looking at this American society. I remember, during the time I was in West Africa—some of you may be here today because I don't know what it's all about, but I know I can tell you the truth, too—it was a lot of people there that was called the PIAA. "What are you doing over here? Who are you trying to please?"

I said, "All you criticize us when you at home and you're worried to death when we try to find out about our own people." I said, "If we had been treated as human beings in America, you wouldn't be trailing us now to find out what we is trying to do over here."

But this is something we going to have to learn to do and quit saying that we are free in America when I know we are not free. You are not free in Harlem. The people are not free in Chicago, because I've been there, too. They are not free in Philadelphia, because I've been there, too. And when you get it over with all the way around, some of the places is a Mississippi in disguise. And we want a change. And we hope you support us in this challenge that we'll begin on the 4th of January. And give us what support that you can.

Thank you.

Testimony Before the Credentials Committee, Democratic National Convention

Democratic National Convention, August 22, 1964,
Atlantic City, New Jersey

Mr. Chairman, and to the Credentials Committee, my name is Mrs. Fannie Lou Hamer, and I live at 626 East Lafayette Street, Ruleville, Mississippi, Sunflower County, the home of Senator James O. Eastland, and Senator Stennis.

It was the 31st of August in 1962 that eighteen of us traveled twenty-six miles to the county courthouse in Indianola to try to register to become first-class citizens.

We was met in Indianola by policemen, Highway Patrolmen, and they only allowed two of us in to take the literacy test at the time. After we had taken this test and started back to Ruleville, we was held up by the City Police and the State Highway Patrolmen and carried back to Indianola where the bus driver was charged that day with driving a bus the wrong color.

After we paid the fine among us, we continued on to Ruleville, and Reverend Jeff Sunny carried me four miles in the rural area where I had worked as a timekeeper and sharecropper for eighteen years. I was met there by my children, who told me that the plantation owner was angry because I had gone down to try to register.

After they told me, my husband came, and said the plantation owner was raising Cain because I had tried to register. Before he quit talking the plantation owner came and said, "Fannie Lou, do you know—did Pap tell you what I said?"

And I said, "Yes, sir."

He said, "Well I mean that." He said, "If you don't go down and withdraw your registration, you will have to leave." Said, "Then if you go down and withdraw," said, "you still might have to go because we are not ready for that in Mississippi."

And I addressed him and told him and said, "I didn't try to register for you. I tried to register for myself."

I had to leave that same night.

On the 10th of September 1962, sixteen bullets was fired into the home of Mr. and Mrs. Robert Tucker for me. That same night two girls were shot in Ruleville, Mississippi. Also Mr. Joe McDonald's house was shot in.

And June the 9th, 1963, I had attended a voter registration workshop; was returning back to Mississippi. Ten of us was traveling by the Continental Trailway bus. When we got to Winona, Mississippi, which is Montgomery County, four of the people got off to use the washroom, and two of the people—to use the restaurant—two of the people wanted to use the washroom.

The four people that had gone in to use the restaurant was ordered out. During this time I was on the bus. But when I looked through the window and saw they had rushed out I got off of the bus to see what had happened. And one of the ladies said, "It was a State Highway Patrolman and a Chief of Police ordered us out."

I got back on the bus and one of the persons had used the washroom got back on the bus, too.

As soon as I was seated on the bus, I saw when they began to get the five people in a highway patrolman's car. I stepped off of the bus to see what was happening and somebody screamed from the car that the five workers was in and said, "Get that one there." When I went to get in the car, when the man told me I was under arrest, he kicked me.

I was carried to the county jail and put in the booking room. They left some of the people in the booking room and began to place us in cells. I was placed in a cell with a young woman called Miss Ivesta Simpson. After I was placed in the cell I began to hear sounds of licks and screams, I could hear the sounds of licks and horrible screams. And I could hear somebody say, "Can you say, 'yes, sir,' nigger? Can you say 'yes, sir'?"

And they would say other horrible names. She would say, "Yes, I can say 'yes, sir.'" "So, well, say it."

She said, "I don't know you well enough."

They beat her, I don't know how long. And after a while she began to pray, and asked God to have mercy on those people.

And it wasn't too long before three white men came to my cell. One of these men was a State Highway Patrolman and he asked me where I was from. I told him Ruleville and he said, "We are going to check this."

They left my cell and it wasn't too long before they came back. He said, "You are from Ruleville all right," and he used a curse word. And he said, "We are going to make you wish you was dead."

I was carried out of that cell into another cell where they had two Negro prisoners. The State Highway Patrolmen ordered the first Negro to take the blackjack.

The first Negro prisoner ordered me, by orders from the State Highway Patrolman, for me to lay down on a bunk bed on my face.

I laid on my face and the first Negro began to beat. I was beat by the first Negro until he was exhausted. I was holding my hands behind me at that time on my left side, because I suffered from polio when I was six years old.

After the first Negro had beat until he was exhausted, the State Highway Patrolman ordered the second Negro to take the blackjack.

The second Negro began to beat and I began to work my feet, and the State Highway Patrolman ordered the first Negro who had beat me to sit on my feet—to keep me from working my feet. I began to scream and one white man got up and began to beat me in my head and tell me to hush.

One white man—my dress had worked up high—he walked over and pulled my dress—I pulled my dress down and he pulled my dress back up.

I was in jail when Medgar Evers was murdered.

All of this is on account of we want to register, to become first-class citizens. And if the Freedom Democratic Party is not seated now, I question America. Is this America, the land of the free and the home of the brave, where we have to sleep with our telephones off the hooks because our lives be threatened daily, because we want to live as decent human beings, in America?

Thank you.

17

Shirley Chisholm

1924–2005

Shirley Chisholm stands without peer in American electoral politics. In 1968, she was the first Black woman elected to the U.S. Congress. Her 1972 presidential run inspired other Black women, such as Barbara Lee, to seek elected office. Self-defined as "unbought and unbossed," Chisholm exhorted people to "aim high." Her vision, integrity, tenacity, skill, and daring set the standard for women of all races, particularly Black women, in politics.

Declaring Presidential Bid

January 25, 1972, Brooklyn, New York

I stand before you today as a candidate for the Democratic nomination for the presidency of the United States of America. I am not the candidate of black America, although I am black and proud. I am not the candidate of the women's movement of this country, although I am a woman, and I'm equally proud of that. I am not the candidate of any political body or backpacks or special interests.

I stand here now without endorsement from many big-name politicians or celebrities or any other kind of prop. I do not intend to offer to you the tired and bled clichés that for too long have been affecting part of our political life.

I am the candidate of the people of America.

Fellow Americans, we have looked in vain to the Nixon administration for the courage, the spirit, the character and the words to lift us, to bring out the best in us, to rekindle in each of us our faith in the American dream. Yet all that we have received in return, just below the smooth exercise in political manipulation, deceit and deception, callousness and indifference to our individual problems, and the disgusting playing of divisive politics. Pinning the young against the old. Labor against management. North against South. Black against white.

The abiding concern of this administration has been one of political expediency rather than the needs of man's nature. The president has broken his promises to us and therefore [*unintelligible*] to our trust and confidence in him.

I cannot believe—I cannot believe that this administration would have ever been elected four years ago if we had known then what we know today.

But we are entering—we are entering a new era in which we must as Americans demand facture and size in our national leadership. Leadership that is fresh, leadership that is open, and leadership bringing perspective to the problem of all Americans.

I have faith in the American people. I believe that we are smart enough to correct our mistakes. I believe we are intelligent enough to recognize the talent, energy and dedication which all Americans, including women and minorities, have to offer.

I know from my travels to the cities and small towns of America that we have a back potential which can and must be put to constructive use in getting this great nation together. I know that millions of Americans from all walks of life agree with me, that leadership does not mean putting the ear to the ground, to follow public opinion, but to have the vision of one necessary and the courage to make it possible.

Americans all over are demanding a new sensibility, a new philosophy of government from Washington. Instead of sending spies to snoop on participants on Earth Day, I would welcome the efforts of concerned citizens of all ages to stop the abuse of our environment.

Instead of watching a football game on television while young people beg for the attention of their president concerning our actions abroad, I would encourage them to speak out, organize for peaceful change and vote in November. Instead of mocking efforts to control the huge amounts of money given to political candidates by the rich and the powerful, I would provide certain limits on such amounts and encourage all the people of this nation to contribute small sums to the candidates of their choice.

Instead of calculating the political cost of this or that policy, and a [*unintelligible*] of this or that group, depending on whether that group voted for me in 1958, I would remind all Americans at this hour of the words of Abraham Lincoln, "a house divided cannot stand."

We Americans—we Americans are all fellow countrymen. One day confronting the judgment of history in our country. We are all God's children, and a bit of each of us is a [*unintelligible*] of the most powerful, general or corporate millionaire.

Those of you—those of you who were locked outside of the convention hall in 1968, those of you who can now vote for the first time, those of you who agree with me that the institutions of this country belong to all of the people who inhabit it. Those of you who have been neglected, left out, ignored, forgotten or shunned for whatever reason. Give me your help at this hour. Join me in an effort to reshape our society and regain control of our destiny, as we go down the Chisholm Trail of 1972.

For the Equal Rights Amendment

Congressional floor speech, U.S. House of Representatives, August 10, 1970, Washington, DC

Mr. Speaker, House Joint Resolution 264, before us today, which provides for equality under the law for both men and women, represents one of the most clear-cut opportunities we are likely to have to declare our faith in the principles that shaped our Constitution. It provides a legal basis for attack on the most subtle, most pervasive, and most institutionalized form of prejudice that exists. Discrimination against women, solely on the basis of their sex, is so widespread that is seems to many persons normal, natural and right.

Legal expression of prejudice on the grounds of religious or political belief has become a minor problem in our society. Prejudice on the basis of race is, at least, under systematic attack. There is reason for optimism that it will start to die with the present, older generation. It is time we act to assure full equality of opportunity to those citizens who, although in a majority, suffer the restrictions that are commonly imposed on minorities, to women.

The argument that this amendment will not solve the problem

of sex discrimination is not relevant. If the argument were used against a civil rights bill, as it has been used in the past, the prejudice that lies behind it would be embarrassing. Of course laws will not eliminate prejudice from the hearts of human beings. But that is no reason to allow prejudice to continue to be enshrined in our laws—to perpetuate injustice through inaction.

The amendment is necessary to clarify countless ambiguities and inconsistencies in our legal system. For instance, the Constitution guarantees due process of law, in the 5th and 14th amendments. But the applicability of due process of sex distinctions is not clear. Women are excluded from some State colleges and universities. In some States, restrictions are placed on a married woman who engages in an independent business. Women may not be chosen for some juries. Women even receive heavier criminal penalties than men who commit the same crime. What would the legal effects of the equal rights amendment really be? The equal rights amendment would govern only the relationship between the State and its citizens—not relationships between private citizens. The amendment would be largely self-executing, that is, and Federal or State laws in conflict would be ineffective one year after date of ratification without further action by the Congress or State legislatures.

Opponents of the amendment claim its ratification would throw the law into a state of confusion and would result in much litigation to establish its meaning. This objection overlooks the influence of legislative history in determining intent and the recent activities of many groups preparing for legislative changes in this direction.

State labor laws applying only to women, such as those limiting hours of work and weights to be lifted would become inoperative unless the legislature amended them to apply to men. As of early 1970 most States would have some laws that would be affected. However, changes are being made so rapidly as a result of title VII of the Civil Rights Act of 1964, it is likely that by the time the equal rights amendment would become effective, no confliction State laws would remain.

In any event, there has for years been great controversy as to the usefulness to women of these State labor laws. There has never been any doubt that they worked a hardship on women who need or want to work overtime and on women who need or want better paying jobs, and there has been no persuasive evidence as to how many women benefit from the archaic policy of the laws. After the Delaware hours law was repealed in 1966, there were no complaints from women to any of the State agencies that might have been approached.

Jury service laws not making women equally liable for jury service would have been revised. The selective service law would have to include women, but women would not be required to serve in the Armed Forces where they are not fitted any more than men are required to serve. Military service, while a great responsibility, is not without benefits, particularly for young men with limited education or training.

Since October 1966, 246,000 young men who did not meet the normal mental or physical requirements have been given opportunities for training and correcting physical problems. This opportunity is not open to their sisters. Only girls who have completed high school and meet high standards on the educational test can volunteer. Ratification of the amendment would not permit application of higher standards to women.

Survivorship benefits would be available to husbands of female workers on the same basis as to wives of male workers. The Social Security Act and the civil service and military service retirement acts are in conflict. Public schools and universities could not be limited to one sex and could not apply different admission standards to men and women. Laws requiring longer prison sentences for women than men would be invalid, and equal opportunities for rehabilitation and vocational training would have to be provided in public correctional institutions. Different ages of majority based on sex would have to be harmonized. Federal, State, and other governmental bodies would be obligated to follow nondiscriminatory practices in all aspects of employment, including public school teachers and State university and college faculties.

What would be the economic effects of the equal rights amendment? Direct economic effects would be minor. If any labor laws applying only to women still remained, their amendment or repeal would provide opportunity for women in better-paying jobs in manufacturing. More opportunities in public vocational and graduate schools for women would also tend to open up opportunities in better jobs for women.

Indirect effects could be much greater. The focusing of public attention on the gross legal, economic, and social discrimination against women by hearings and debates in the Federal and State legislatures would result in changes in attitude of parents, educators, and employers that would bring about substantial economic changes in the long run.

Sex prejudice cuts both ways. Men are oppressed by the requirements of the Selective Service Act, by enforced legal guardianship of minors, and by alimony laws. Each sex, I believe, should be liable when necessary to serve and defend this country. Each has a responsibility for the support of children.

There are objections raised to wiping out laws protecting women workers. No one would condone exploitation. But what does sex have to do with it. Working conditions and hours that are harmful to women are harmful to men; wages that are unfair for women are unfair for men. Laws setting employment limitations on the basis of sex are irrational, and the proof of this is their inconsistency from State to State. The physical characteristics of men and women are not fixed, but cover two wide spans that have a great deal of overlap. It is obvious, I think, that a robust woman could be more fit for physical labor than a weak man. The choice of occupation would be determined by individual capabilities, and the rewards for equal works should be equal.

This is what it comes down to: artificial distinctions between persons must be wiped out of the law. Legal discrimination between the sexes is, in almost every instance, founded on outmoded views of society and the pre-scientific beliefs about psychology and physiology. It is time to sweep away these relics of the past and set further generations free of them. Federal agencies and institutions responsible for the enforcement of equal opportunity laws need the authority of a Constitutional amendment. The 1964 Civil Rights Act and the 1963 Equal Pay Act are not enough; they are limited in their coverage—for instance, one excludes teachers, and the other leaves out administrative and professional women. The Equal Employment Opportunity Commission has not proven to be an adequate device, with its power limited to investigation, conciliation, and recommendation to the Justice Department. In its cases involving sexual discrimination, it has failed in more than one-half. The Justice Department has been even less effective. It has intervened in only one case involving discrimination on the basis of sex, and this was on a procedural point. In a second case, in which both sexual and racial discrimination were alleged, the racial bias charge was given far greater weight.

Evidence of discrimination on the basis of sex should hardly have to be cited here. It is in the Labor Department's employment and salary figures for anyone who is still in doubt. Its elimination will involve so many changes in our State and Federal laws that, without the authority and impetus of this proposed amendment, it will perhaps take another 194 years. We cannot be parties to continuing a delay. The time is clearly now to put this House on record for the fullest expression of that equality of opportunity which our founding fathers professed. They professed it, but they did not assure it to their daughters, as they tried to do for their sons.

The Constitution they wrote was designed to protect the rights of white, male citizens. As there were no black Founding Fathers, there were no founding mothers—a great pity, on both counts. It is not too late to complete the work they left undone. Today, here, we should start to do so.

In closing I would like to make one point. Social and psychological effects will be initially more important than legal or economic results. As Leo Kanowitz has pointed out: Rules of law that treat the sexes per se inevitably produce far-reaching effects upon social, psychological and economic aspects of male-female relations beyond the limited confines of legislative chambers and courtrooms. As long as organized legal systems, at once the most respected and most feared of social institutions, continue to differentiate sharply, in treatment or in words, between men and women on the basis of irrelevant and artificially created distinctions, the likelihood of men and women coming to regard one another primarily as fellow human beings and only secondarily as representatives of another sex will continue to be remote. When men and women are prevented from recognizing one another's essential humanity by sexual prejudices, nourished by legal as well as social institutions, society as a whole remains less than it could otherwise become.

18

Maya Angelou

1928–2014

A stellar example of Black women creating productive and inspiring lives, the poet and writer Maya Angelou not only knew "why the caged bird sings" (the title of her bestselling memoir) but also set free the aspirations of countless people in the arts and in social justice movements. As a civil rights activist, Angelou worked with Rev. Dr. Martin Luther King Jr. at the Southern Christian Leadership Conference and also with Malcolm X. Among the highlights of her distinguished career was delivering her stirring poem "On the Pulse of Morning" at the 1993 inauguration of President Bill Clinton and being awarded the Presidential Medal of Freedom by Barack Obama in 2010.

On the Pulse of Morning

Inauguration of President Bill Clinton, January 20, 1993, Washington, DC

A Rock, A River, A Tree
Hosts to species long since departed,
Marked the mastodon,
The dinosaur, who left dry tokens
Of their sojourn here
On our planet floor,
Any broad alarm of their hastening doom
Is lost in the gloom of dust and ages.

But today, the Rock cries out to us, clearly, forcefully,
Come, you may stand upon my
Back and face your distant destiny,
But seek no haven in my shadow,
I will give you no hiding place down here.

You, created only a little lower than
The angels, have crouched too long in
The bruising darkness,

Have lain too long
Face down in ignorance,
Your mouths spilling words

Armed for slaughter.
The Rock cries out to us today, you may stand upon me,
But do not hide your face.

Across the wall of the world,
A River sings a beautiful song, It says
Come rest here by my side.

Each of you a bordered country,
Delicate and strangely made proud,
Yet thrusting perpetually under siege.
Your armed struggles for profit
Have left collars of waste upon
My shore, currents of debris upon my breast.
Yet, today I call you to my riverside,
If you will study war no more. Come,
Clad in peace and I will sing the songs
The Creator gave to me when I and the
Tree and the rock were one.
Before cynicism was a bloody sear across your
Brow and when you yet knew you still
Knew nothing.
The River sang and sings on.

There is a true yearning to respond to
The singing River and the wise Rock.
So say the Asian, the Hispanic, the Jew
The African, the Native American, the Sioux,
The Catholic, the Muslim, the French, the Greek
The Irish, the Rabbi, the Priest, the Sheikh,

The Gay, the Straight, the Preacher,
The privileged, the homeless, the Teacher.
They all hear
The speaking of the Tree.

They hear the first and last of every Tree
Speak to humankind today. Come to me, here beside the River.
Plant yourself beside the River.

Each of you, descendant of some passed
On traveller, has been paid for.
You, who gave me my first name, you
Pawnee, Apache, Seneca, you
Cherokee Nation, who rested with me, then
Forced on bloody feet,
Left me to the employment of
Other seekers–desperate for gain,
Starving for gold.
You, the Turk, the Arab, the Swede, the German, the Eskimo, the Scot,
You the Ashanti, the Yoruba, the Kru, bought
Sold, stolen, arriving on a nightmare
Praying for a dream.
Here, root yourselves beside me.
I am that Tree planted by the River,
Which will not be moved.
I, the Rock, I the River, I the Tree
I am yours–your Passages have been paid.
Lift up your faces, you have a piercing need
For this bright morning dawning for you.
History, despite its wrenching pain,
Cannot be unlived, but if faced
With courage, need not be lived again.

Lift up your eyes upon
This day breaking for you.
Give birth again
To the dream.

Women, children, men,
Take it into the palms of your hands.
Mold it into the shape of your most
Private need. Sculpt it into
The image of your most public self.
Lift up your hearts
Each new hour holds new chances
For a new beginning.
Do not be wedded forever
To fear, yoked eternally
To brutishness.

The horizon leans forward,
Offering you space to place new steps of change.
Here, on the pulse of this fine day
You may have the courage
To look up and out and upon me, the
Rock, the River, the Tree, your country.
No less to Midas than the mendicant.
No less to you now than the mastodon then.

Here on the pulse of this new day
You may have the grace to look up and out
And into your sister's eyes, and into
Your brother's face, your country
And say simply
Very simply
With hope—
Good morning.

19

Lorraine Hansberry

1930-1965

Lorraine Hansberry achieved literary fame during a brief and shining career as a playwright. Her landmark work, *A Raisin in the Sun*, opened on Broadway in 1959—the first Broadway production by a Black woman. This gripping drama captured the challenges and ironies of an African American family searching for the American dream. Until her untimely death at thirty-four, Hansberry used her celebrity to speak up for civil and human rights.

The Black Revolution and the White Backlash

Forum at Town Hall sponsored by the Association of Artists for Freedom, June 15, 1964, New York, New York

How do you talk about 300 years in four minutes? [*sighs, laughter, applause*] Was it ever so apparent we need this dialogue? [*laughter, applause*]

I wrote a letter to the *New York Times* recently which didn't get printed, which is getting to be my rapport with the *New York Times*. They said that it was too personal. What it concerned itself with was, I was in a bit of a stew over the stall-in, because when the stall-in was first announced, I said, "Oh, My God, now everybody's gone crazy, you know, tying up traffic. What's the matter with them? You know. Who needs it?" And then I noticed the reaction, starting in Washington and coming on up to New York among what we are all here calling the white liberal circles which was something like, you know, "You Negroes act right or you're going to ruin everything we're trying to do." [*laughter*] And that got me to thinking more seriously about the strategy and the tactic that the stall-in intended to accomplish.

And so I sat down and wrote a letter to the *New York Times* about the fact that I am of a generation of Negroes that comes after a whole lot of other generations and my father, for instance, who was, you know, real "American" type American: successful businessman, very civic-minded and so forth; was the sort of American who put a great deal of money, a great deal of his really extraordinary talents and a great deal of passion into everything that we say is the American way of going after goals. That is to say that he moved his family into a restricted area where no Negroes were supposed to live and then proceeded to fight the case in the courts all the way to the Supreme Court of the United States. And this cost a great deal of money. It involved the assistance of NAACP attorneys and so on and this is the way of struggling that everyone says is the proper way to do and it eventually resulted in a decision against restrictive covenants which is very famous, *Hansberry v. Lee*. And that was very much applauded.

But the problem is that Negroes are just as segregated in the city of Chicago now as they were then [*laughter*] and my father died a disillusioned exile in another country. That is the reality that I'm faced with when I get up and I read that some Negroes my own age and younger say that we must now lie down in the streets, tie up traffic, stop ambulances, do whatever we can, take to the hills if necessary with some guns and fight back, you see. This is the difference.

And I wrote to the *Times* and said, you know, "Can't you understand that this is the perspective from which we are now speaking? It isn't as if we got up today and said, you know, 'what can we do to irritate America?'" [*laughter*] you know. It's because that since 1619, Negroes have tried every method of communication, of transformation of their situation from petition to the vote, everything. We've tried it all. There isn't anything that hasn't been exhausted. Isn't it rather remarkable that we can talk about a people who were publishing newspapers while they were still in slavery in 1827, you see?

We've been doing everything, writing editorials, Mr. Wechsler, for a long time, you know. [*applause*]

And now the charge of impatience is simply unbearable. I would like to submit that the problem is that, yes, there is a problem about white liberals. I think there's something horrible that Norman Podhoretz, for instance, can sit down and write the kind of trash that he did at this hour. [*applause*] That is to say that a distinguished American thinker can literally say that he is more disturbed at the sight of a mixed couple or that anti-Semitism from Negroes—and anti-Semitism from anybody is horrible and disgusting and I don't care where it comes from—but anti-Semitism, somehow, from a Negro apparently upsets him more than it would from a German fascist, you see. This was the implication of what really gets to him. [*applause*] Well, you have to understand that when we are confronted with that, we wonder who we are talking to and how far we are going to go.

The problem is we have to find some way with these dialogues to show and to encourage the white liberal to stop being a liberal and become an American radical. [*applause*] I think that then it wouldn't—when that becomes true, some of the really eloquent things that were said before about the basic fabric of our society, which after all, is the thing which must be changed, you know, [*applause*] to really solve the problem, you know. The basic organization of American society is the thing that has Negroes in the situation that they are in and never let us lose sight of it.

When we then talk with that understanding, it won't be so difficult for people like Mr. Wechsler, whose sincerity I wouldn't dream of challenging, when I say to him [*laughter*]—his sincerity is one thing, I don't have to agree with his position. But it wouldn't be so difficult for me to say, well, now, when someone uses the term "cold war liberal" that it is entirely different, you see, the way that you would assess the Vietnamese war and the way that I would because

I can't believe . . . [*applause*] I can't believe that anyone who is given what an American Negro is given—you know, our viewpoint—can believe that a government which has at its disposal a Federal Bureau of Investigation which cannot ever find the murderers of Negroes and by that method . . . [*applause*] and shows that it cares really very little about American citizens who are black, really are over somewhere fighting a war for a bunch of other colored people, you know, [*laughter*] several thousand miles—you just have a different viewpoint.

This is why we want the dialogue, to explain that to you, you see. It isn't a question of patriotism and loyalty. My brother fought for this country, my grandfather before that and so on and that's all a lot of nonsense when we criticize. The point is that we have a different viewpoint because, you know, we've been kicked in the face so often and the vantage point of Negroes is entirely different and these are some of the things we're trying to say. I don't want to go past my time. Thank you. [*applause*]

20

Myrlie Evers-Williams

1933–

Myrlie Evers-Williams is a civil rights activist who founded the first NAACP office in Mississippi, with her husband Medgar Evers. In 1963, Medgar was murdered by a white supremacist; it took thirty years to bring the murderer to justice. Evers-Williams has dedicated her life to the cause of justice, serving in many prominent roles—including as chair of the board of the NAACP. In January 2103, she delivered the invocation at the second inauguration of President Barack Obama.

Invocation at the 2013 Presidential Inauguration

Inauguration of President Barack Obama, January 21, 2013, Washington, DC

America, we are here, our nation's Capitol on this January the 21st 2013, the inauguration of our 45th[1] president Barack Obama. We come at this time to ask blessings upon our leaders, the president, vice president, members of Congress, all elected and appointed officials of the United States of America. We are here to ask blessings upon our armed forces, blessings upon all who contribute to the essence of the American spirit, the American dream. The opportunity to become whatever our mankind, womankind, allows us to be. This is the promise of America.

As we sing the words of belief, "this is my country," let us act upon the meaning that everyone is included. May the inherent dignity and inalienable rights of every woman, man, boy and girl be honored. May all your people, especially the least of these, flourish in our blessed nation. One hundred fifty years after the Emancipation

1 President Obama is the 44th president of the United States of America.

Proclamation and 50 years after the March on Washington, we celebrate the spirit of our ancestors, which has allowed us to move from a nation of unborn hopes and a history of disenfranchised [votes] to today's expression of a more perfect union. We ask, too, almighty that where our paths seem blanketed by [throngs] of oppression and riddled by pangs of despair we ask for your guidance toward the light of deliverance. And that the vision of those that came before us and dreamed of this day, that we recognize that their visions still inspire us.

They are a great cloud of witnesses unseen by the naked eye but all around us thankful that their living was not in vain. For every mountain you gave us the strength to climb. Your grace is pleaded to continue that climb for America and the world. We now stand beneath the shadow nation's Capitol whose golden dome reflects the unity and democracy of one nation, indivisible with liberty and justice for all. Approximately four miles from where we are assembled the hallowed remains of men and women rest in Arlington Cemetery. They who believed, fought and died for this country. May their spirit infuse our being to work together with respect, enabling us to continue to build this nation, and in so doing we send a message to the world that we are strong, fierce in our strength, and ever vigilant in our pursuit of freedom. We ask that you grant our president the will to act courageously but cautiously when confronted with danger and to act prudently but deliberately when challenged by adversity. Please continue to bless his efforts to lead by example in consideration and favor of the diversity of our people.

Bless our families all across this nation.

We thank you for this opportunity of prayer to strengthen us for the journey through the days that lie ahead.

We invoke the prayers of our grandmothers, who taught us to pray, "God make me a blessing." Let their spirit guide us as we claim the spirit of old.

There's something within me that holds the reins. There's something within me that banishes pain. There's something within me I cannot explain. But all I know America, there is something within. There is something within.

In Jesus' name and the name of all who are holy and right we pray. Amen.

21

Audre Lorde

1934–1992

Audre Lorde was one of the most influential poets of her generation, a woman who boldly described herself as "Black, lesbian, mother, warrior, poet." Her work was a forerunner of what we now call *intersectionality*. "I cannot be simply a Black person and not be a woman too," she once remarked in an interview, "nor can I be a woman without being a lesbian." The author of numerous collections of poetry and prose, Lorde was also a professor at John Jay College and Hunter College, in New York City. Lorde won many awards and accolades throughout her career and served as poet laureate of New York from 1991 to 1992.

Age, Race, Class, and Sex: Women Redefining Difference

Paper delivered at the Copeland Colloquium, Amherst College, April 1980; published in *Sister Outsider: Essays and Speeches*

Much of Western European history conditions us to see human differences in simplistic opposition to each other: dominant/subordinate, good/bad, up/down, superior/inferior. In a society where the good is defined in terms of profit rather than in terms of human need, there must always be some group of people who, through systematized oppression, can be made to feel surplus, to occupy the place of the dehumanized inferior. Within this society, that group is made up of Black and Third World people, working-class people, older people, and women.

As a forty-nine-year-old Black lesbian feminist socialist mother of two, including one boy, and a member of an interracial couple, I usually find myself a part of some group defined as other, deviant, inferior, or just plain wrong. Traditionally, in American society, it is the members of oppressed, objectified groups who are expected to stretch out and bridge the gap between the actualities of our lives and the consciousness of our oppressor. For in order to survive, those of us for whom oppression is as American as apple pie have always had to be watchers, to become familiar with the language and manners of the oppressor, even sometimes adopting them for some illusion of protection. Whenever the need for some pretense of communication arises, those who profit from our oppression call upon us to share our knowledge with them. In other words, it is the responsibility of the oppressed to teach the oppressors their mistakes. I am responsible for educating teachers who dismiss my children's culture in school. Black and Third World people are expected to educate white people as to our humanity. Women are expected to educate men. Lesbians and gay men are expected to educate the heterosexual world. The oppressors maintain their position and evade responsibility for their own actions. There is a constant drain of energy which might be better used in redefining ourselves and devising realistic scenarios for altering the present and constructing the future.

Institutionalized rejection of difference is an absolute necessity in a profit economy which needs outsiders as surplus people. As members of such an economy, we have *all* been programmed to respond to the human differences between us with fear and loathing and to handle that difference in one of three ways: ignore it, and if that is not possible, copy it if we think it is dominant, or destroy it if we think it is subordinate. But we have no patterns for relating across our human differences as equals. As a result, those differences have been misnamed and misused in the service of separation and confusion.

Certainly there are very real differences between us of race, age, and sex. But it is not those differences between us that are separating us. It is rather our refusal to recognize those differences, and to examine the distortions which result from our misnaming them and their effects upon human behavior and expectation.

Racism, the belief in the inherent superiority of one race over all oth-

ers and thereby the right to dominance. Sexism, the belief in the inherent superiority of one sex over the other and thereby the right to dominance. Ageism. Heterosexism. Elitism. Classism.

It is a lifetime pursuit for each one of us to extract these distortions from our living at the same time as we recognize, reclaim, and define those differences upon which they are imposed. For we have all been raised in a society where those distortions were endemic within our living. Too often, we pour the energy needed for recognizing and exploring difference into pretending those differences are insurmountable barriers, or that they do not exist at all. This results in a voluntary isolation, or false and treacherous connections. Either way, we do not develop tools for using human difference as a springboard for creative change within our lives. We speak not of human difference, but of human deviance.

Somewhere, on the edge of consciousness, there is what I call a *mythical* norm, which each one of us within our hearts knows "that is not me." In America, this norm is usually defined as white, thin, male, young, heterosexual, Christian, and financially secure. It is with this mythical norm that the trappings of power reside within this society. Those of us who stand outside that power often identify one way in which we are different, and we assume that to be the primary cause of all oppression, forgetting other distortions around difference, some of which we ourselves may be practising. By and large within the women's movement today, white women focus upon their oppression as women and ignore differences of race, sexual preference, class, and age. There is a pretense to a homogeneity of experience covered by the word *sisterhood* that does not in fact exist.

Unacknowledged class differences rob women of each other's energy and creative insight. Recently a women's magazine collective made the decision for one issue to print only prose, saying poetry was a less "rigorous" or "serious" art form. Yet even the form our creativity takes is often a class issue. Of all the art forms, poetry is the most economical. It is the one which is the most secret, which requires the least physical labor, the least material, and the one which can be done between shifts, in the hospital pantry, on the subway, and on scraps of surplus paper. Over the last few years, writing a novel on tight finances, I came to appreciate the enormous differences in the material demands between poetry and prose. As we reclaim our literature, poetry has been the major voice of poor, working class, and Colored women. A room of one's own may be a necessity for writing prose, but so are reams of paper, a typewriter, and plenty of time. The actual requirements to produce the visual arts also help determine, along class lines, whose art is whose. In this day of inflated prices for material, who are our sculptors, our painters, our photographers? When we speak of a broadly based women's culture, we need to be aware of the effect of class and economic differences on the supplies available for producing art.

As we move toward creating a society within which we can each flourish, ageism is another distortion of relationship which interferes without vision. By ignoring the past, we are encouraged to repeat its mistakes. The "generation gap" is an important social tool for any repressive society. If the younger members of a community view the older members as contemptible or suspect or excess, they will never be able to join hands and examine the living memories of the community, nor ask the all important question, "Why?" This gives rise to a historical amnesia that keeps us working to invent the wheel every time we have to go to the store for bread.

We find ourselves having to repeat and relearn the same old lessons over and over that our mothers did because we do not pass on what we have learned, or because we are unable to listen. For instance, how many times has this all been said before? For another, who would have believed that once again our daughters are allowing their bodies to be hampered and purgatoried by girdles and high heels and hobble skirts? Ignoring the differences of race between women and the implications of those differences presents the most serious threat to the mobilization of women's joint power.

As white women ignore their built-in privilege of whiteness and define woman in terms of their own experience alone, then women of Color become "other," the outsider whose experience and tradition is too "alien" to comprehend. An example of this is the signal absence of the experience of women of Color as a resource for women's studies courses. The literature of women of Color is seldom included in women's literature courses and almost never in other literature courses, nor in women's studies as a whole. All too often, the excuse given is that the literatures of women of Color can only be taught by Colored women, or that they are too difficult to understand, or that classes cannot "get into" them because they come out of experiences that are "too different." I have heard this argument presented by white women of otherwise quite clear intelligence, women who seem to have no trouble at all teaching and reviewing work that comes out of the vastly different experiences of Shakespeare, Moliere, Dostoyefsky, and Aristophanes. Surely there must be some other explanation.

This is a very complex question, but I believe one of the reasons white women have such difficulty reading Black women's work is because of their reluctance to see Black women as women and different from themselves. To examine Black women's literature effectively requires that we be seen as whole people in our actual complexities—as individuals, as women, as human—rather than as one of those problematic but familiar stereotypes provided in this society in place of genuine images of Black women. And I believe this holds true for the literatures of other women of Color who are not Black.

The literatures of all women of Color recreate the textures of our lives, and many white women are heavily invested in ignoring the real differences. For as long as any difference between us means one of us must be inferior, then the recognition of any difference must be fraught with guilt. To allow women of Color to step out of stereotypes is too guilt provoking, for it threatens the complacency of those women who view oppression only in terms of sex.

Refusing to recognize difference makes it impossible to see the different problems and pitfalls facing us as women.

Thus, in a patriarchal power system where white skin privilege is a major prop, the entrapments used to neutralize Black women and white women are not the same. For example, it is easy for Black women to be used by the power structure against Black men, not because they are men, but because they are Black. Therefore, for Black women, it is necessary at all times to separate the needs of the oppressor from our own legitimate conflicts within our communities. This same problem does not exist for white women. Black women and men have shared racist oppression and still share it, although in different ways. Out of that shared oppression we have developed joint defenses and joint vulnerabilities to each other that are not duplicated in the white community, with the exception of the relationship between Jewish women and Jewish men.

On the other hand, white women face the pitfall of being seduced into joining the oppressor under the pretense of sharing power. This possibility does not exist in the same way for women of Color. The tokenism that is sometimes extended to us is not an invitation to join power; our racial "otherness" is a visible reality that makes that quite clear. For white women there is a wider range of pretended choices and rewards for identifying with patriarchal power and its tools.

Today, with the defeat of ERA, the tightening economy, and increased conservatism, it is easier once again for white women to believe the dangerous fantasy that if you are good enough, pretty enough, sweet enough, quiet enough, teach the children to behave, hate the right people, and marry the right men, then you will be allowed to co-exist with patriarchy in relative peace, at least until a man needs your job or the neighborhood rapist happens along. And true, unless one lives and loves in the trenches it is difficult to remember that the war against dehumanization is ceaseless.

But Black women and our children know the fabric of our lives is stitched with violence and with hatred, that there is no rest. We do not deal with it only on the picket lines, or in dark midnight alleys, or in the places where we dare to verbalize our resistance. For us, increasingly, violence weaves through the daily tissues of our living—in the supermarket, in the classroom, in the elevator, in the clinic and the schoolyard, from the plumber, the baker, the saleswoman, the bus driver, the bank teller, the waitress who does not serve us.

Some problems we share as women, some we do not. You fear your children will grow up to join the patriarchy and testify against you, we fear our children will be dragged from a car and shot down in the street, and you will turn your backs upon the reasons they are dying.

The threat of difference has been no less blinding to people of Color. Those of us who are Black must see that the reality of our lives and our struggle does not make us immune to the errors of ignoring and misnaming difference. Within Black communities where racism is a living reality, differences among us often seem dangerous and suspect. The need for unity is often misnamed as a need for homogeneity, and a Black feminist vision mistaken for betrayal of our common interests as a people. Because of the continuous battle against racial erasure that Black women and Black men share, some Black women still refuse to recognize that we are also oppressed as women, and that sexual hostility against Black women is practiced not only by the white racist society, but implemented within our Black communities as well. It is a disease striking the heart of Black nationhood, and silence will not make it disappear. Exacerbated by racism and the pressures of powerlessness, violence against Black women and children often becomes a standard within our communities, one by which manliness can be measured. But these woman-hating acts are rarely discussed as crimes against Black women.

As a group, women of Color are the lowest paid wage earners in America. We are the primary targets of abortion and sterilization abuse, here and abroad. In certain parts of Africa, small girls are still being sewed shut between their legs to keep them docile and for men's pleasure. This is known as female circumcision, and it is not a cultural affair as the late Jomo Kenyatta insisted, it is a crime against Black women.

Black women's literature is full of the pain of frequent assault, not only by a racist patriarchy, but also by Black men. Yet the necessity for and history of shared battle have made us, Black women, particularly vulnerable to the false accusation that anti-sexist is anti-Black. Meanwhile, womanhating as a recourse of the powerless is sapping strength from Black communities, and our very lives. Rape is on the increase, reported and unreported, and rape is not aggressive sexuality, it is sexualized aggression. As Kalamu ya Salaam, a Black male writer points out, "As long as male domination exists, rape will exist. Only women revolting and men made conscious of their responsibility to fight sexism can collectively stop rape."

Differences between ourselves as Black women are also being misnamed and used to separate us from one another. As a Black lesbian feminist comfortable with the many different ingredients of my identity, and a woman committed to racial and sexual freedom from oppression, I find I am constantly being encouraged to pluck out some one aspect of myself and present this as the meaningful whole, eclipsing or denying the other parts of self. But this is a destructive and fragmenting way to live. My fullest concentration of energy is available to me only when I integrate all the parts of who I am, openly, allowing power from particular sources of my living to flow back and forth freely through all my different selves, without the restrictions of externally imposed definition. Only then can I bring myself and my energies as a whole to the service of those struggles which I embrace as part of my living.

A fear of lesbians, or of being accused of being a lesbian, has led many Black women into testifying against themselves. It has led some of us into destructive alliances, and others into despair and isolation. In the white women's communities, heterosexism is sometimes a result of identifying with the white patriarchy, a rejection of that interdependence between women-identified women which allows the self to be, rather than to be used in the service of men. Sometimes it reflects a die-hard belief in the protective coloration of heterosexual relationships, sometimes a self-hate which all women have to fight against, taught us from birth.

Although elements of these attitudes exist for all women, there are particular resonances of heterosexism and homophobia among Black women. Despite the fact that woman-bonding has a long and honorable history in the African and African American communities, and despite the knowledge and accomplishments of many strong and creative women-identified Black women in the political, social and cultural fields, heterosexual Black women often tend to ignore or discount the existence and work of Black lesbians. Part of this attitude has come from an understandable terror of Black male attack within the close confines of Black society, where the punishment for any female self-assertion is still to be accused of being a lesbian and therefore unworthy of the attention or support of the scarce Black male. But part of this need to misname and ignore Black lesbians comes from a very real fear that openly women-identified Black women who are no longer dependent upon men for their self-definition may well reorder our whole concept of social relationships.

Black women who once insisted that lesbianism was a white woman's problem now insist that Black lesbians are a threat to Black nationhood, are consorting with the enemy, are basically un-Black. These accusations, coming from the very women to whom we look for deep and real understanding, have served to keep many Black lesbians in hiding, caught between the racism of white women and the homophobia of their sisters. Often, their work has been ignored, trivialized, or misnamed, as with the work of Angelina Grimke, Alice Dunbar-Nelson, Lorraine Hansberry. Yet women-bonded women have always been some part of the power of Black communities, from our unmarried aunts to the amazons of Dahomey.

And it is certainly not Black lesbians who are assaulting women and raping children and grandmothers on the streets of our communities.

Across this country, as in Boston during the spring of 1979 following the unsolved murders of twelve Black women, Black lesbians are spearheading movements against violence against Black women.

What are the particular details within each of our lives that can be scrutinized and altered to help bring about change? How do we redefine difference for all women? It is not our differences which separate women, but our reluctance to recognize those differences and to deal effectively with the distortions which have resulted from the ignoring and misnaming of those differences.

As a tool of social control, women have been encouraged to recognize only one area of human difference as legitimate, those differences which exist between women and men. And we have learned to deal across those differences with the urgency of all oppressed subordinates. All of us have had to learn to live or work or coexist with men, from our fathers on. We have recognized and negotiated these differences, even when this recognition only continued the old dominant/subordinate mode of human relationship; where the oppressed must recognize the masters' difference in order to survive.

But our future survival is predicated upon our ability to relate within equality. As women, we must root out internalized patterns of oppression within ourselves if we are to move beyond the most superficial aspects of social change. Now we must recognize differences among women who are our equals, neither inferior nor superior, and devise ways to use each other's difference to enrich our visions and our joint struggles. The future of our earth may depend upon the ability of all women to identify and develop new definitions of power and new patterns of relating across difference. The old definitions have not served us, nor the earth that supports us. The old patterns, no matter how cleverly rearranged to imitate progress, still condemn us to cosmetically altered repetitions of the same old exchanges, the same old guilt, hatred, recrimination, lamentation, and suspicion.

For we have, built into all of us, old blueprints of expectation and response, old structures of oppression, and these must be altered at the same time as we alter the living conditions which are a result of those structures. For the master's tools will never dismantle the master's house.

As Paulo Freire shows so well in *The Pedagogy of the Oppressed*, the true focus of revolutionary change is never merely the oppressive situations which we seek to escape, but that piece of the oppressor which is planted deep within each of us, and which knows only the oppressors' tactics, the oppressors' relationships.

Change means growth, and growth can be painful. But we sharpen self-definition by exposing the self in work and struggle together with those whom we define as different from ourselves, although sharing the same goals. For Black and white, old and young, lesbian and heterosexual women alike, this can mean new paths to our survival.

We have chosen each other
and the edge of each others battles
the war is the same
if we lose
someday women's blood will congeal
upon a dead planet
if we win
there is no telling
we seek beyond history
for a new and more possible meeting.

22

Barbara Jordan

1936–1996

Congresswoman Barbara Jordan's name is synonymous with skilled, impassioned oratory grounded in historical perspective and advocacy for civil rights. She served on the Judiciary Committee of the U.S. House of Representatives, gaining in reputation and stature after her powerful speech in favor of the 1974 impeachment of President Richard M. Nixon for violating the Constitution. Legislation she sponsored in 1975 expanded the Voting Rights Act of 1965 to include more people of color. Her keynote speech at the 1976 Democratic National Convention made her the first woman and the first African American to have that honor.

1976 Democratic National Convention Keynote Address

Democratic National Convention, July 12, 1976,
New York, New York

Thank you ladies and gentlemen for a very warm reception.

It was one hundred and forty-four years ago that members of the Democratic Party first met in convention to select a Presidential candidate. Since that time, Democrats have continued to convene once every four years and draft a party platform and nominate a Presidential candidate. And our meeting this week is a continuation of that tradition. But there is something different about tonight. There is something special about tonight. What is different? What is special?

I, Barbara Jordan, am a keynote speaker.

A lot of years passed since 1832, and during that time it would have been most unusual for any national political party to ask that a Barbara Jordan to deliver a keynote address. But tonight here I am. And I feel that notwithstanding the past that my presence here is one additional bit of evidence that the American Dream need not forever be deferred.

Now that I have this grand distinction what in the world am I supposed to say? I could easily spend this time praising the accomplishments of this party and attacking the Republicans—but I don't choose to do that. I could list the many problems which Americans have. I could list the problems which cause people to feel cynical, angry, frustrated: problems which include lack of integrity in government; the feeling that the individual no longer counts; the reality of material and spiritual poverty; the feeling that the grand American experiment is failing or has failed. I could recite these problems, and then I could sit down and offer no solutions. But I don't choose to do that either. The citizens of America expect more. They deserve and they want more than a recital of problems.

We are a people in a quandary about the present. We are a people in search of our future. We are a people in search of a national community. We are a people trying not only to solve the problems of the present, unemployment, inflation, but we are attempting on a larger scale to fulfill the promise of America. We are attempting to fulfill our national purpose, to create and sustain a society in which all of us are equal.

Throughout our history, when people have looked for new ways to solve their problems, and to uphold the principles of this nation, many times they have turned to political parties. They have often turned to the Democratic Party. What is it? What is it about the Democratic Party that makes it the instrument the people use when they search for ways to shape their future? Well I believe the answer to that question lies in our concept of governing. Our concept of governing is derived from our view of people. It is a concept deeply rooted in a set of beliefs firmly etched in the national conscience of all of us.

Now what are these beliefs? First, we believe in equality for all and privileges for none. This is a belief that each American regardless of background has equal standing in the public forum—all of us. Because we believe this idea so firmly, we are an inclusive rather than an exclusive party. Let everybody come! I think it no accident that most of those emigrating to America in the 19th century identified with the Democratic Party. We are a heterogeneous party made up of Americans of diverse backgrounds. We believe that the people are the source of all governmental power; that the authority of the people is to be extended, not restricted.

This can be accomplished only by providing each citizen with every opportunity to participate in the management of the government. They must have that, we believe. We believe that the government which represents the authority of all the people, not just one interest group, but all the people, has an obligation to actively—underscore actively—seek to remove those obstacles which would block individual achievement—obstacles emanating from race, sex, economic condition. The government must remove them, seek to remove them.

We are a party of innovation. We do not reject our traditions, but we are willing to adapt to changing circumstances, when change we must. We are willing to suffer the discomfort of change in order to achieve a better future. We have a positive vision of the future founded on the belief that the gap between the promise and reality of America can one day be finally closed.

We believe that.

This, my friends, is the bedrock of our concept of governing. This is a part of the reason why Americans have turned to the Democratic Party. These are the foundations upon which a national community can be built. Let's all understand that these guiding principles cannot be discarded for short-term political gains. They represent what this country is all about. They are indigenous to the American idea. And these are principles which are not negotiable.

In other times, I could stand here and give this kind of exposition on the beliefs of the Democratic Party and that would be enough. But today that is not enough. People want more. That is not sufficient reason for the majority of the people of this country to vote Democratic. We have made mistakes. We realize that. In our haste to do all things for all people, we did not foresee the full consequences of our actions. And when the people raised their voices, we didn't hear. But our deafness was only a temporary condition, and not an irreversible condition.

Even as I stand here and admit that we have made mistakes, I still believe that as the people of America sit in judgment on each party, they will recognize that our mistakes were mistakes of the heart. They'll recognize that.

And now we must look to the future. Let us heed the voice of the people and recognize their common sense. If we do not, we not only blaspheme our political heritage, we ignore the common ties that bind all Americans. Many fear the future. Many are distrustful of their leaders, and believe that their voices are never heard. Many seek only to satisfy their private work wants. To satisfy their private interests. But this is the great danger America faces. That we will cease to be one nation and become instead a collection of interest groups: city against suburb, region against region, individual against individual. Each seeking to satisfy private wants. If that happens, who then will speak for America? Who then will speak for the common good?

This is the question which must be answered in 1976.

Are we to be one people bound together by common spirit, sharing in a common endeavor; or will we become a divided nation? For all of its uncertainty, we cannot flee the future. We must not become the new Puritans and reject our society. We must address and master the future together. It can be done if we restore the belief that we share a sense of national community, that we share a common national endeavor. It can be done.

There is no executive order; there is no law that can require the American people to form a national community. This we must do as individuals, and if we do it as individuals, there is no President of the United States who can veto that decision.

As a first step, we must restore our belief in ourselves. We are a generous people so why can't we be generous with each other? We need to take to heart the words spoken by Thomas Jefferson:

Let us restore to social intercourse that harmony and affection without which liberty and even life are but dreary things. A nation is formed by the willingness of each of us to share in the responsibility for upholding the common good. A government is invigorated when each of us is willing to participate in shaping the future of this nation. In this election year we must define the common good and begin again to shape a common future. Let each person do his or her part. If one citizen is unwilling to participate, all of us are going to suffer. For the American idea, though it is shared by all of us, is realized in each one of us.

And now, what are those of us who are elected public officials supposed to do? We call ourselves public servants but I'll tell you this: We as public servants must set an example for the rest of the nation. It is hypocritical for the public official to admonish and exhort the people to uphold the common good if we are derelict in upholding the common good. More is required of public officials than slogans and handshakes and press releases. More is required. We must hold ourselves strictly accountable. We must provide the people with a vision of the future.

If we promise as public officials, we must deliver. If we as public officials propose, we must produce. If we say to the American people it is time for you to be sacrificial; sacrifice. If the public official says that, we [public officials] must be the first to give. We must be. And again, if we make mistakes, we must be willing to admit them. We have to do that. What we have to do is strike a balance between the idea that government should do everything and that idea, the belief, that government ought to do nothing. Strike a balance. Let there be no illusions about the difficulty of forming this kind of a national community. It's tough, difficult, not easy. But a spirit of harmony will survive in America only if each of us remembers that we share a common destiny. If each of us remembers when self-interest and bitterness seem to prevail that we share a common destiny.

I have confidence that we can form this kind of national community.

I have confidence that the Democratic Party can lead the way.

I have that confidence.

We cannot improve on the system of government handed down to us by the founders of the Republic. There is no way to improve upon that. But what we can do is to find new ways to implement that system and realize our destiny.

Now, I began this speech by commenting to you on the uniqueness of a Barbara Jordan making a keynote address. Well I am going to close my speech by quoting a Republican President and I ask you that as you listen to these words of Abraham Lincoln, relate them to the concept of a national community in which every last one of us participates:

"As I would not be a slave, so I would not be a master. This expresses my idea of Democracy. Whatever differs from this, to the extent of the difference, is no Democracy."

Thank you.

Proceedings on the Impeachment of Richard Nixon

Opening statement to the House Judiciary Committee, July 25, 1974, Washington, DC

Mr. Chairman, I join my colleague Mr. Rangel in thanking you for giving the junior members of this committee the glorious opportunity of sharing the pain of this inquiry.

Mr. Chairman, you are a strong man, and it has not been easy but we have tried as best we can to give you as much assistance as possible.

Earlier today we heard the beginning of the Preamble to the Constitution of the United States, "We, the people". It is a very eloquent beginning. But when that document was completed, on the seventeenth of September in 1787, I was not included in that "We, the people". I felt somehow for many years that George Washington and Alexander Hamilton just left me out by mistake. But through the process of amendment, interpretation, and court decision I have finally been included in "We, the people".

Today I am an inquisitor. I believe hyperbole would not be fictional and would not overstate the solemnness that I feel right now.

My faith in the Constitution is whole, it is complete, it is total. I am not going to sit here and be an idle spectator to the diminution, the subversion, the destruction of the Constitution.

Who can so properly be the inquisitors for the nation as the representatives of the nation themselves? The subject of its jurisdiction are those offenses which proceed from the misconduct of public men. That is what we are talking about. In other words, the jurisdiction comes from the abuse of violation of some public trust. It is wrong, I suggest, it is a misreading of the Constitution for any member here to assert that for a member to vote for an article of impeachment means that that member must be convinced that the president should be removed from office. The Constitution doesn't say that.

The powers relating to impeachment are an essential check in the hands of this body, the legislature, against and upon the encroachment of the executive. In establishing the division between the two branches of the legislature, the House and the Senate, assigning to the one the right to accuse and to the other the right to judge, the framers of this Constitution were very astute. They did not make the accusers and the judges the same person.

We know the nature of impeachment. We have been talking about it awhile now. It is chiefly designed for the president and his high ministers to somehow be called into account. It is designed to "bridle" the executive if he engages in excesses. It is designed as a method of national inquest into the public men. The framers confined in the congress the power if need be, to remove the president in order to strike a delicate balance between a president swollen with power and grown tyrannical, and preservation of the independence of the executive.

The nature of impeachment is a narrowly channeled exception to the separation-of-powers maxim; the federal convention of 1787 said that. It limited impeachment to high crimes and misdemeanors and discounted and opposed the term "maladministration." "It is to be used only for great misdemeanors," so it was said in the North Carolina ratification convention. And in the Virginia ratification convention: "We do not trust our liberty to a particular branch. We need one branch to check the others."

The North Carolina ratification convention: "No one need be afraid that officers who commit oppression will pass with immunity." "Prosecutions of impeachments will seldom fail to agitate the passions of the whole community," said Hamilton in the Federalist Papers, no. 65. "And to divide it into parties more or less friendly or inimical to the accused." I do not mean political parties in that sense.

The drawing of political lines goes to the motivation behind impeachment; but impeachment must proceed within the confines of the constitutional term "high crimes and misdemeanors." Of the impeachment process, it was Woodrow Wilson who said that "nothing short of the grossest offenses against the plain law of the land will suffice to give them speed and effectiveness. Indignation so great as to overgrow party interest may secure a conviction; but nothing else can." Common sense would be revolted if we engaged upon this process for insurance, campaign finance reform, housing, environmental protection, energy sufficiency, mass transportation. Pettiness cannot be allowed to stand in the face of such overwhelming problems. So today we are not being petty. We are trying to be big because the task we have before us is a big one.

This morning, in a discussion of the evidence, we were told that the evidence which purports to support the allegations of misuse of the CIA by the president is thin. We are told that that evidence is insufficient. What that recital of the evidence this morning did not include is what the president did know on June 23, 1972. The president did know that it was Republican money, that it was money from the Committee for the Re-Election of the President, which was found in the possession of one of the burglars arrested on June 17.

What the president did know on June 23 was the prior activities of E. Howard Hunt, which included his participation in the break-in of Daniel Ellsberg's psychiatrist, which included Howard Hunt's participation in the Dita Beard ITT affair, which included Howard Hunt's fabrication of cables designed to discredit the Kennedy administration.

We were further cautioned today that perhaps these proceedings ought to be delayed because certainly there would be new evidence forthcoming from the president. The committee subpoena is outstanding, and if the president wants to supply that material, the committee sits here.

The fact is that yesterday, the American people waited with great anxiety for eight hours, not knowing whether their president would obey an order of the Supreme Court of the United States. At this point I would like to juxtapose a few of the impeachment criteria with some of the president's actions.

Impeachment criteria: James Madison, from the Virginia ratification convention. "If the president be connected in any suspicious manner with any person and there be grounds to believe that he will shelter him, he may be impeached."

We have heard time and time again that the evidence reflects payment to the defendants of money. The president had knowledge that these funds were being paid and that these were funds collected for the 1972 presidential campaign. We know that the president met with Mr. Henry Petersen twenty-seven times to discuss matters related to Watergate and immediately thereafter met with the very persons who were implicated in the information Mr. Petersen was receiving and transmitting to the president. The words are "if the president be connected in any suspicious manner with any person and there be grounds to believe that he will shelter that person, he may be impeached."

Justice Story: "Impeachment is intended for occasional and extraordinary cases where a superior power acting for the whole people is put into operation to protect their rights and rescue their liberties from violations."

We know about the Huston plan. We know about the break-in of the psychiatrist's office. We know that there was absolute complete direction in August 1971 when the president instructed Ehrlichman to "do whatever is necessary." This instruction led to a surreptitious entry into Dr. Fielding's office. "Protect their rights." "Rescue their liberties from violation."

The South Carolina ratification convention impeachment criteria: those are impeachable "who behave amiss or betray their public trust." Beginning shortly after the Watergate break-in and continuing to the present time, the president has engaged in a series of public statements and actions designed to thwart the lawful investigation by government prosecutors. Moreover, the president has made public announcements and assertions bearing on the Watergate case which the evidence will show he knew to be false.

These assertions, false assertions, impeachable, those who misbehave. Those who "behave amiss or betray their public trust." James Madison again at the Constitutional Convention: "A president is impeachable if he attempts to subvert the Constitution."

The Constitution charges the president with the task of taking care that the laws be faithfully executed, and yet the president has counseled his aides to commit perjury, willfully disregarded the secrecy of grand jury proceedings, concealed surreptitious entry, attempted to compromise a federal judge while publicly displaying his cooperation with the processes of criminal justice.

"A president is impeachable if he attempts to subvert the Constitution."

If the impeachment provision in the Constitution of the United States will not reach the offenses charged here, then perhaps that eighteenth century Constitution should be abandoned to a twentieth-century paper shredder. Has the president committed offenses and planned and directed and acquiesced in a course of conduct which the Constitution will not tolerate? That is the question. We know that. We know the question. We should now forthwith proceed to answer the question. It is reason, and not passion, which must guide our deliberations, guide our debate, and guide our decision.

23

Marian Wright Edelman

1939–

Marian Wright Edelman is founder and president emerita of the Children's Defense Fund (CDF), often referred to as the nation's strongest advocate for children and families. Prior to founding CDF in 1973, she directed the NAACP Legal Defense and Educational Fund in Jackson, Mississippi, and became counsel to Martin Luther King Jr.'s Poor People's Campaign in 1968. Among many other distinctions, Edelman was the first Black woman to be admitted to the bar in the state of Mississippi.

Standing Up for the World's Children: Leave No Child Behind

State of the World Forum, October 1996, San Francisco, California

---

I am deeply honoured to participate in this State of the World Forum and thank those who brought us together.

We are living in a time of unbearable dissonance between promise and performance; between good politics and good policy; between professed and practiced family values; between racial creed and racial deed; between calls for community and rampant individualism and greed; and between our capacity to prevent and alleviate human deprivation and disease and our political and spiritual will to do so.

Something is awry when the net worth of the world's 358 richest people equals the combined income of the poorest 45 percent—or 2.3 billion people—of the world's population, and when the per capita income gap between the developed and developing worlds has tripled since 1960. Something is awry when, in the United States, 23,000 families lived on less income in 1993 than one entertainment industry executive. These facts are not acts of God but of men and can be changed. We also are living at an incredible moral moment in history—Few human beings are blessed to anticipate or experience the beginning of a new century and millennium. How will we say thanks for the life, earth, nations, and children God has entrusted to our care? What legacies, principles, values, and deeds will we stand for and send to the future through our children to their children and to a spiritually confused, balkanized, and violent world desperately hungering for moral leadership and community?

How will progress be measured over the next thousand years if we survive them? By the kill power and number of weapons of destruction we can produce and traffic at home and abroad, or by our willingness to shrink, indeed destroy, the prison of violence constructed in the name of peace and security? Will we be remembered in this last part of the 20th century by how many material things we can manufacture, advertise, sell, and consume, or by our rediscovery of more lasting, non-material measures of success—a new Dow Jones for the purpose and quality of life in our families, neighborhoods, cities, national, and world communities. By how rapidly technology and corporate mergermania can render human beings and human work obsolete, or by our search for a better balance between corporate profits and corporate caring for children, families, and communities? Will we be remembered by how much a few at the top can get at the expense of the many at the bottom and in the middle, or by our struggle for a concept of enough for all? Will we be remembered by the glitz, style, and banality of too much of our culture in McLuhan's electronic global village or by the substance of our efforts to rekindle an ethic of caring, community, and justice in a world driven too much by money, technology, and weaponry?

The answers lie in the values we stand for and in the actions we take today. What an opportunity for good or evil we personally and collectively hold in our hands as parents, citizens, religious, community, and political leaders; and—for those Americans among us—as titular world leader in this post-Cold War and post-industrial era on the cusp of the third millennium.

A thousand years ago the United States was not even a dream. Copernicus and Galileo had not told us the earth was round or revolved around the sun. Gutenberg's Bible had not been printed, Wycliffe had not translated it into English, and Martin Luther had not tacked his theses on the church door. The Magna Carta did not exist, Chaucer's and Shakespeare's tales had not been spun, and Bach's, Beethoven's, and Mozart's miraculous music had not been created to inspire, soothe, and heal our spirits. European serfs struggled in bondage while many African and Asian empires flourished in independence. Native Americans peopled America, free of slavery's blight, and Hitler's holocaust had yet to show the depths human evil can reach when good women and men remain silent or indifferent.

A thousand years from now, will civilization remain and humankind Survive? Will America's dream be alive, be remembered, and be worth remembering? Will the United States be a blip or a beacon in history? Can our founding principle "that all men are created equal" and "are endowed by their Creator with certain inalienable rights" withstand the test of time, the tempests of politics, and become deed and not just creed for EVERY child? Is American's dream big enough for every fifth child who is poor, every sixth child who is Black, every seventh child who is Hispanic, and every eighth child who is mentally or physically challenged? Is our world's dream big enough for all of the children God has sent as messengers of hope?

Can our children become the healing agents of our national and world transformation and future spiritual and economic salvation? Edmond McDonald wrote that "when God wants an important thing done in this world or a wrong righted, He goes about it in a very singular way. He doesn't release thunderbolts or stir up earthquakes. God simply has a tiny baby born, perhaps of a very humble home, perhaps of a very humble mother. And God puts the idea or purpose into the mother's heart. And she puts it in the baby's mind, and then God waits. The great events of this world are not battles and elections and earthquakes and thunderbolts. The great events are babies, for each child comes with the message that God is not yet discouraged with humanity, but is still expecting goodwill to become incarnate in each human life." And so God produced a Gorbachev and a Mandela and a Harriet Tubman and an Eleanor Roosevelt and an Arias and each of us to guide the earth towards peace rather than conflict.

I believe that protecting today's children, tomorrow's Mandelas and Mother Theresas, is the moral and common sense litmus test of our humanity in a world where millions of child lives are ravaged by the wars, neglect, abuse, and racial, ethnic, religious, and class divisions of adults.

The state of the world's children today represents both a colossal triumph and failure for humankind. Over the last fifteen years, through the "child survival revolution", UNICEF and WHO, working with governments and nongovernmental organizations, have saved tens of millions of child lives—perhaps the greatest humanitarian act in history. Rising developing world's child immunization rates (from 25 percent to nearly 80 percent); oral rehydration therapy to combat diarrhea; advances against vitamin A deficiency; the iodization of salt (which eliminates iodine deficiency disorders and much preventable mental retardation); the distinct possibility that polio, like small pox, will soon become extinct; and the increasingly effective campaign against guinea worm disease, are among the greatest yet most invisible human triumphs of the 20th Century. Together they prevent as many as 5 million child deaths a year.

These triumphs are overshadowed, however, by our failure to

prevent nearly 8 million other child deaths each year. The shortfall is not in vaccine efficacy, health worker willingness, or parental concern but primarily in the priorities and commitment in many developing and developed countries to meet the needs of the more than 120 million children born poor each year. And the shortfall is in our failure to provide the 30–40 billion additional dollars a year needed to reach the year 2000 child health and development goals set by the nations of the world in 1990. UNICEF says the world spends more than this on playing golf and that Europeans spend more on cigarettes. $30–40 billion is far less than defense budget cuts around the world since the Cold War ended. Indeed, U.S. spending (in real inflation adjusted dollars) on arms exceeds the amount spent during the average year of the Cold war. In the U.S. we are spending $30 million an hour on national defense—more on the military every 14 hours than we spend annually on child abuse prevention and treatment programs; more on the military every 29 hours than on summer jobs for unemployed youth; and more in just 5 hours on the military than we invest in early Head Start for poor children under three.

Little or none of the wholly inadequate "peace dividend" has been invested in urgently needed child and human development. While child deaths from disease have fallen dramatically, child deaths in wars and civil conflicts have risen. In the last decade, 2 million children have been killed and 4 1/2 million have been disabled in wars. Warring sides increasingly target civilian populations and so-called leaders recognize the pliability of children as soldiers. Lighter and simpler weapons like AK-47s and M-16s have given still-growing children greater firepower just as the cancerous spread of small, cheap "Saturday Night special" handguns have done in my country. In the ultimate adult abuse and corruption of childhood's innocence, children have become engaged in war as soldiers and as civilian targets. In over 25 countries in the last decade, children under 16 and as young as 6 have fought in wars and the U.S. gun manufacturers have targeted women and children as a consumer market. And the deadly fruits of war in the form of landmines daily turn childhood dreams into nightmares in many parts of the world.

Epidemic violence coupled with growing inequality among and within many nations; persistent poverty, especially in Africa and in the U.S.; widespread hunger and malnutrition in South Asia and elsewhere; and disparate education levels between boys and girls (although investing in education of girls can increase incomes, free women from subjection, improve child health and nutrition, increase marriages, and lower birth rates) keep us from realizing Martin Luther King, Jr.'s vision of a beloved community. It is not only the developing world that has a child survival and development crisis. The stagnation, retrogression, and lack of political and moral will to invest in children and families in the developed nations of the world must be addressed. Strong communities rest on strong families. Yet in the United States, and to varying degrees throughout the developed world, young families with children are struggling with falling wages and income. The number of children growing up in single-parent families has skyrocketed; and teen pregnancy and parenting rates remain stubbornly high. Lengthening life spans, fewer children per family, and more single-parent families all mean that parents and grandparents living with children are a shrinking share of the electorate, and the political power needed for voteless children is eroding. Decreasing adult time for child nurturing, coupled with child corrupting content from powerful modern communications technologies like television, pose ominous problems for the world and the United States and threaten our leadership role in the 21st century world. Among industrialized nations, the United States ranks:

1st in military technology and exports;

1st in Gross Domestic Product (GNP);
1st in defense expenditures; and,
1st in the number of millionaires and billionaires

But we rank worst in the number of children killed by guns among industrialized nations and have twice the rate of teen births as England, and five times the rates in France, Italy, and other Western European nations. Our children rank 7th in science and 12th in mathematics achievement among 15 nations (as 13-year-olds); 16th in living standards among our poorest fifth children; 18th in 18 industrialized countries in the gap between rich and poor children; 18th in infant mortality (27th if we compare only Black infant mortality); and 19th in low birth weight rates. Most tragically, the morally unthinkable killing of children has become routine in Boston, Bosnia, and Burundi, in New York city and Rwanda, and is increasing. In the U.S., since 1979, more than 50,000 American children have been killed by guns in our homes, schools, and neighborhoods in a civil war on and among our own young. This is more child gun deaths than all America's battlefield casualties during the entire Vietnam War. Although we are the world's leading military power, we permit a classroom full of children to be killed violently every two days from guns—one child every hour and a half. White children constituted more than half the 5,751 children killed by guns in 1993. Guns kill more American preschool children each year than law enforcement officers or active duty military personnel in the line of duty. The 2,221 Black children and youths murdered by firearms in 1993 were almost twice the total number of gun homicides in Australia, Belgium, Canada, the United Kingdom, France, Germany, Holland, Norway, Spain, Switzerland, and Finland combined. More toddlers and preschool school children were murdered in 1993 than citizens of all ages in Japan, Switzerland, Holland, England and Wales.

Our nation responds to this tragedy not by taking guns out of the hands of children and those who kill them, and not by giving parents the jobs, child care, and health support they need to give children the home environments; and not by investing adequately in quality schools, and after-school and summer activities that will keep children safer, engaged, and give them hopes for their futures, but by decreasing child and family investments, putting more children in adult jails, and making the citizenry fear children by branding them "predators" and "teen terrorists." The recently enacted welfare repeal bill will slash over $50 billion from low-income families with children (most of whom work and are not on welfare, are legal immigrants or disabled); consign a million more children to poverty and sharply cut family and child nutrition benefits for 14 million children. Our leaders did not demand any sacrifices from corporate welfare recipients and Pentagon contractors. Our challenge is to build a citizen movement so strong that no political leader of any party will be able to do this again—even in an election year.

What Do We Do?

First: we must affirm the sanctity of each child. (Jewish Midrash). When Jesus Christ invited the little children to come unto Him, He did not invite only rich, middle class, White, male, children without disabilities, from two parent families, or our own children to come. He welcomed all children. And so must we. All great faiths place a priority on child protection. Our challenge is to reflect this priority every day in our families, communities, and professional lives, and in our private sector and governmental policies.

Two: We must build strong politics and climate for child investment that cuts across race and class, and appeal to self-interest as well as conscience. And we must combat the myths that it is only poor or minority children or those in developing nations who are afflicted by the breakdown of moral, family, and community values throughout our world today. The pollution of our airwaves, air, food, and water; growing economic insecurity among middle-class children and young families; rampant drug and alcohol abuse; teen pregnancy; and domestic violence among rich; middle-class, and poor alike; AIDS; random gun and terrorist violence; resurging racial, ethnic, and gender intolerance in our places of learning, work, and worship; and the crass, empty materialism of too much of our culture, threaten every child. Affluenza and lack of moral purpose are more dangerous viruses than influenza for millions of America's and the world's children.

Third: we must stop adult hypocrisy and live what we preach. Our children do what we do and not just what we say. Each of us must conduct regular personal audits and make sure we are a part of the solution and not a part of the problem our children face. If we tell or snicker at racial or gender jokes or acquiesce in practices that demean other human beings, then we are a part of the problem. If we are violent, our children will be violent. If we abuse drugs—including alcohol and tobacco—while telling our children not to, then we are contributing to our overly addicted societies. If we do not engage in regular service to others, our children will absorb our selfishness. We must also preach better what we practice if it is good.

Fourth: conduct a community audit to see if schools, religious, and other community institutions are providing children and youths positive alternatives to the streets, to drug dealers, and gangs, and to the relentless cultural messages glamourizing irresponsible sex, and excessive violence and materialism. And we must celebrate the majority of children who are beating the odds rather than just publicizing the minority who get into trouble. We must insist that the media provide a better balance between good and bad news. A key to this is personalizing child suffering. We must take opinion and political leaders on site visits to see the children and families behind the statistics and policies. And we must show them solutions as well as problems. We must disseminate widely the things that do work so that the public will know that positive change is possible and occurring.

Fifth: monitor and conduct regular national audits of how private sector and governmental policies impact on children and engage in strong, systematic advocacy to meet child needs first.

Children don't vote but adults who do must stand up and vote for them. While personal responsibility, moral example, and private charity are crucial, so are jobs, decent wages, child care, health care, clean air, water, and public safety that government must ensure, in collaboration with employers. All the soup kitchens and homeless shelters in the world cannot substitute for community and economic development which provide jobs with decent wages, and dignity. But we will not achieve adequate child and family investments in the U.S. without a massive, moral movement to redirect the leadership and budget priorities of our nation.

A lot of people, including CDF, have been seeding and watering this movement for over two decades. On June 1, 1996, it reached a crucial new stage when, in just four months, 3,800 organizations and over 300,000 Americans of every race, age, faith, state, and ideology stood together at the Lincoln memorial. Thousands more stood in 133 local rallies throughout the country. We committed to putting our children first as parents, grandparents, citizens, and community leaders and insist our private and public sector leaders do so. Children's Action Teams are engaging in follow-up action in 46 states and laying the foundation for the long overdue grassroots movement needed to protect our children. In July, 125,000 Massachusetts children got health coverage when citizens and state legislators overrode a governor's veto of a pending child health bill. Thousands more individuals are volunteering in child-serving programs, monitoring child policies, and tutoring and mentoring children. On October 18–20, thousands of congregations of all faiths will lift up child needs during annual Children Sabbaths celebrations; and children's summits and rallies are taking place in California, New York, and Michigan in this month alone. Next June 1st we plan a Virtual Stand for Children Day which I hope our friends around the world will join in. Every state, city, and congressional district and community need a well-trained band of leaders committed to lifting up child needs and mobilizing a critical mass of citizens to ensure all children a Healthy, Fair, Safe, and Moral Start in life. Leadership development, especially among youth and local community leaders, must be a high priority for us all.

Sixth: all the nations of the world can use the International Convention of the Rights of the Child to promote child well being. Promulgated in the early 1990s to lift up children's needs, the Convention gives children a comprehensive set of social, economic, civil, and political rights to be protected against discrimination, child labor, and sexual exploitation; to speech and participation commensurate with their age; to adequate health care, food, shelter, and other items of subsistence; and to a range of other basics we adults take for granted. And the Convention does all this while recognizing the paramount importance of parents and family. No human rights treaty in history has been ratified so quickly by so many countries. To date, 167 countries have ratified and only four (Oman, Somalia, the United Arab Emirate, and the Cook Islands) have neither signed nor ratified the Convention. And only two—I'm embarrassed to say they are the United States and Switzerland—have signed but have not ratified this Convention.

Nevertheless, the 1990 World Summit for Children at the United Nations and the Convention on the Rights of the Child have helped consolidate the presence of children and young people in political and social debate in international bodies and dozens of countries around the world. For decades to come, the Convention will be an essential framework for national and international action for children.

Let me end with a prayer:

O GOD OF ALL CHILDREN O God of the children of Somalia, Sarajevo, South Africa, and South Carolina, Of Albania, Alabama, Bosnia, and Boston, Of Cracow and Cairo, Chicago and Croatia, Help us to love and respect and protect them all. O God of black and brown and white and Albino children and those all mixed together, Of children who are rich and poor and in between, Of children who speak English and Russian and Hmong and Spanish and languages our ears cannot discern, Help us to love and respect and protect them all. O God of the child prodigy and child prostitute, of the child of rapture and the child of rape. Of run or thrown away children who struggle every day without parent or place or friend or future, Help us to love and respect and protect them all. O God of the children who can walk and talk and hear and see and sing and dance and jump and play and of children who wish they could but they can't, Of children who are loved and unloved, wanted and unwanted, Help us to love and respect and protect them all. O God of beggar, beaten, abused, neglected, homeless, AIDS, drug, and hunger-ravaged children, Of children who are emotionally and physically and mentally fragile, and of children who rebel and ridicule, torment and taunt, Help us to love and respect and protect them all. O God of children of destiny and of despair, of war and of peace, Of disfigured, diseased, and dying children, Of children without hope and of children with hope to spare and to share, Help us to love and respect and protect them all.

24

Angela Y. Davis

1944-

Angela Davis's long history of activism and her controversial imprisonment in the early 1970s sometimes overshadow the fact that she is a scholar and educator of immense distinction. Her groundbreaking books include *Women, Race, and Class*; *Are Prisons Obsolete?*; and *Freedom Is a Constant Struggle*—all of them contributing to her searing and prophetic analysis of politics and racism. She is a distinguished professor emerita at the University of California, Santa Cruz.

The Liberation of Our People

Black Panther rally in Bobby Hutton Park (aka DeFremery Park), November 12, 1969, Oakland, California

Yeah, I'd just like to say that I like being called sister much more than professor and I've continually said that if my job—if keeping my job means that I have to make any compromises in the liberation struggle in this country, then I'll gladly leave my job. This is my position.

Now there has been a lot of debate in the left sector of the anti-war movement as to what the orientation of that movement should be. And I think there are two main issues at hand. One group of people feels that the movement, the anti-war movement ought to be a single issue movement, the cessation of the war in Vietnam. They do not want to relate it to the other kinds and forms of repression that are taking place here in this country. There's another group of people who say that we have to make those connections. We have to talk about what's happening in Vietnam as being a symptom of something that's happening all over the world, of something that's happening in this country. And in order for the anti-war movement to be effective, it has to link up with the struggle for black and brown liberation in this country with the struggle of exploited white workers. Now I think we should ask ourselves why that first group of people want the anti-war movement to be a single issue movement. Somehow they feel that it's necessary to tone down the political content of that movement in order to attract as many people as possible. They think that mere numbers will be enough in order to affect this government's policy. But I think we have to talk about the political content. We have to talk about the necessity to raise the level of consciousness of the people who are involved in that movement. And if you analyze the war in Vietnam, first of all it ought to become obvious that if the United States Government pulled its troops out of Vietnam that that repression would have to crop up somewhere else. And in fact, we're seeing that as this country is being defeated in Vietnam, more and more acts of repression are occurring here on the domestic scene. And I'd just like to point to the most dramatic one in the last couple of weeks, which is the chaining and gagging of Chairman Bobby Seale and his sentence to four years for Contempt of Court. I think that demonstrates that if the link-up is not made between what's happening in Vietnam and what's happening here we may very well face a period of full-blown fascism very soon.

Now I think there's something perhaps more profound that we ought to point to. This whole economy in this country is a war economy. It's based on the fact that more and more and more weapons are being produced. What happens if the war in Vietnam ceases? How is the economy going to stand unless another Vietnam is created, and who is to determine where that Vietnam is gonna be? It can be abroad, or it can be right here at home, and I think it's becoming evident that that Vietnam is entering the streets of this country. It's becoming evident in all the brutal forms of repression, which we can see everyday of our lives here. And this reminds me, because I think this is very relevant to what's happening in Vietnam that is the military situation in this country. I saw in television last week that the head of the National Guard in California decided that from now on their military activities are gonna be concentrated in three main areas. Now what are these areas? First of all, he says, disruption in minority communities, then he says disruption on the campus, then he says disruption in industrial areas. I think it points to the fact that they are going to begin to use that whole military apparatus in order to put down the resistance in the black and brown community, on the campuses, in the working class communities. I think that they are really preparing for this now. It's evident that the terror is becoming not just isolated instances of police brutality here and there, but that terror is becoming an everyday instrument of the institutions of this country. The Chief of the National Guard said that outright. It's happening in the courts. There is terror in the courts, that judge, whose name is Hoffman proved that he is going to take on the terror in the society and bring it into the courts, that he is going to use what is supposed to be a court of law, justice, equality, whatever you wanna call it in order to meet out all of these, you know fascist acts of repression.

Now something else has been happening in the courts, and I think this is an incident that we all ought to be aware of because it's another instance of terror entering into the courts. Down in San Jose, not too long ago, a young Chicano was on trial and I'd like to read a quote from the transcript, a quote by Judge—I think his name is Chargin, the fascist. He said, "Mexican people, after 13 years of age, it's perfectly all right to go out and act like an animal. Maybe Hitler was right. The animals in our society probably ought to be destroyed because they have no right to live among human beings. You are lower than animals and haven't the right to exist in organized society, just miserable lousy rotten people." Now this is the direct quote from the transcript that's happened within the walls of the courtroom. How can we fail to see that there's an intricate connection between that type of thing between what happened to Bobby Seale, between the unwarranted imprisonment of Huey Newton and what's happening in Vietnam. We are facing a common enemy and that enemy is Yankee Imperialism, which is killing us both here and abroad. Now I think anyone who would try to separate those struggles, anyone who would say that in order to consolidate an anti-war movement, we have to leave all of these other outlying issues out of the picture, is playing right into the hands of the enemy. I mean it's an old saying, I think it's been demonstrated over and over that it's correct that once the people are divided, the enemy will be victorious. We will face defeat. And I think the attempt to isolate what's happening on the domestic scene, from the war in Vietnam is playing right into the hands of the enemy giving him the chance to be victorious.

And I think there's a much more concrete problem. If you talk about the anti-war movement as a separate movement, what happens? What happens if suddenly the troops are pulled out of Vietnam? What happens if Nixon suddenly says we're gonna bring all of the boys home? The people, the thousands, the millions of people who had been involved in that movement would feel as if they had been victorious. I think perhaps a, a number of them would think that they could return home and relish in their victory and say that we have won, completely ignoring the fact that Huey Newton is still in jail, that Erica Huggins and all the other sisters and brothers in Connecticut are still in jail. This is what we are faced with if we cannot make that connection between the international scene and the domestic scene. And I don't think there's any question about it. We can't talk about protesting the genocide of the Vietnamese people without at the same time doing something to stop the genocide that is—that liberation fighters in this country are being subjected to. Now I think we can draw a parallel between what's happening right now and what's—what happened during the 1950s. As the United States Government was being defeated in the Korean War, more and more repression did occur on the domestic scene. The McCarthy witch hunt started. This is the communist party which was the main target of that. I think we have to ask ourselves, why that period served to completely stifle revolutionary activity in this country. People were scared, they run away, they lost their families, they lost their homes. They did not resist. This is the problem. They did not resist. Right now the Black Panther Party is the main target of the repression that's coming down in this society and the Black Panther Party is resisting. And we all ought to talk about standing up and resisting this oppression, resisting the onslaught of fascism in this country. Otherwise, the movement is going to be doomed to failure. I think we can say that if the anti-war movement defends only itself and does not defend liberation fighters in this country, then that movement is going to be doomed to failure, just as we can say also if we in the black liberation movement and the liberation movement for all people in—all oppressed and exploited people in this country, defend only ourselves, then we too will be doomed to failure.

Within the whole liberation struggle in this country, the black liberation struggle and the brown liberation struggle there has continually been the sentiment against the American Imperialist aggressive policies throughout this world because we have been forced to see that the enemy is American imperialism and although we feel it here at home it's being felt perhaps much more brutality in Vietnam, it's being felt in Latin America, it's being felt in Africa, we have to make these connections. [*Inaudible*] has to see that unless it makes that connection, it's going to become irrelevant. And what we have to talk about now is a united force, which sees the liberation of the Vietnamese people as intricately linked up with the liberation of black and brown and exploited white people in this society, and only this kind of a united front, only this kind of a united force can be victorious.

Now I think that there's something else that we ought to consider when we try to analyze what has happened in the anti-war movement. And the anti-war movement hasn't just depended on numbers. It hasn't just depended upon attracting more and more people into the movement regardless of their political orientation. If we remember, the debate a long time ago was whether the anti-war movement or the peace movement then should talk about demanding the cessation of bombing in Vietnam or whether it should talk about withdrawing troops. I think now it's very obvious that you have to talk about withdrawing all American troops from Vietnam. This has occurred only through the process of trying to raise the level of political consciousness of the people who were in that movement. And right now what we have to talk about is not just withdrawing American troops, but also recognizing the South Vietnamese provisional revolutionary government.

Now, I think we have to go a step further. This is what's happening inside the anti-war movement, but we have to take it further. And we have to say that if they, if we demand the immediate withdrawal of American troops in Vietnam [*inaudible*] of the South Vietnamese Provisional Revolutionary Government, then we also have to demand the release of all political prisoners in this country, here. This is what we have to demand. And I think that the liberation struggle here sheds a lot of light on what's happening in Vietnam. It shows us that we can't just push for peace in Vietnam, that we have to talk about also recognizing a revolutionary government. There was a kind of a peace that was obtained right here in this country, in a courtroom, that was the peace which Judge Hoffman forced on Chairman Bobby Seale by coercion, by gagging him and binding him to his chair. This is not the kind of peace that we wanna talk about in Vietnam, the peace in which you have a puppet regime representing the interests of this country in which you have other means of establishing the power of this government in Vietnam.

And I think on a much more personal level, there's some parallels that we can draw. Some very profound parallels I think. And we have to say that Bobby Seale's mother who learned that he had been chained and gagged and that he had been sentenced to four years for contempt of court is no less grieved than an American woman who finds out that her son has been captured in Vietnam, I think we have to say that, that Erica Huggins and Yvonne Carter were no less grieved when they found that their husbands Bunchy and John [*inaudible*] liberation, then an American wife would feel about her husband there, but there is a different political consciousness involved and this is what we have to show the American people today. We have to show the American people that their sons and their husbands are being victimized by American imperialism. They are being forced to go and fight a dirty war in Vietnam. They are victims too and they have to be shown that their true loyalties ought to be with us in the liberation struggle here and with the Vietnamese people in their liberation struggle there. Now Bobby Seale once made a statement at a peace conference in Montreal that the frontline of the battle against racism was in Vietnam. I think we have to ask ourselves what this means because a lot of people may have thought that what this means is that we can depend on the Vietnamese to win our battle here. This is not what he was saying. He was pointing to that inherent connection between what's happening there and what's happening here. And I think we can say and I'm talking from personal experience, I was in Cuba this summer and I met with some representatives of the South Vietnamese Provisional Revolutionary Government and they told us that we were—we, revolutionaries in this country were their most important allies. And not just because we take signs and march in front of the White House saying US Government get out of Vietnam because—rather because we are actively involved in struggling to satisfy the needs of our people in this country and in this way as they point out we are able to internally destroy that monster, which is oppressing people all over the country. I have to admit that I felt a little bit inadequate about that because what he's saying, what the representative of the South Vietnamese Provisional Revolutionary Government was saying is that we are to escalate our struggle in this country, we ought to talk about making more and more demands for the liberation of our people here and this is going to be what they will depend on. This is going to help them in their liberation struggle. Now I think that we ought to talk in the context of this upcoming march here and in Washington about the [*inaudible*] to make simultaneous demands and those demands ought to be immediate withdrawal of US Troops from Vietnam. There ought to be victory for the Vietnamese. There ought to be also recognition of the revolutionary government in South Vietnam and I think this is perhaps most important, we ought to demand the release of political prisoners in this country.

Just one last thing. You know Nixon made a speech on November 3rd, I think it was and he said something that we ought to take heed of, we ought to understand. He said, "Let us understand that the Vietnamese cannot defeat or humiliate our government. Only Americans can do that." I feel that it is our responsibility to fight on all fronts, to fight on all fronts simultaneously to defeat and to humiliate the US Government and all the fascist tactics by which it is repressing liberation fighters in this country.

Thank you very much.

25
Kathleen Cleaver
1945–

Kathleen Cleaver worked with the Student Nonviolent Coordinating Committee and then became involved with the Black Panther Party, where she rose to a leadership position. She went into exile for four years with her then husband, Eldridge Cleaver, who was charged with attempted murder during a police raid in which their friend and Black Panther member Bobby Hutton was killed and two police officers sustained injuries. The Cleavers started the Revolutionary People's Communications Network while in exile. When she returned to the United States, Cleaver graduated with honors from college and law school, becoming a lawyer and a professor. Her books include *Memories of Love and War* and *Liberation, Imagination, and the Black Panther Party: A New Look at the Panthers and Their Legacy*.

Memorial Service for Bobby Hutton

Speech given at memorial service for Bobby Hutton, April 12, 1968, Berkeley, California

---

My first reaction upon finding out about the attack upon the leadership of the Black Panther Party April 6, was that I was glad that I was not a widow for black liberation.

Here I have a message, a telegram that I think I'd like to read, from the widow of our greatest spokesman for black liberation, Malcolm X. It's to the family of Bobby James Hutton, in care of myself.

The question is not will it be nonviolence versus violence, but whether a human being can practice his God-given right to self-defense. Shot down like a common animal, he died a warrior for black liberation. If the generation before him had not been afraid, he perhaps would be alive today.

Remember, like Solomon, there's a time for everything. A time to be born, a time to die, a time to love, a time to hate. A time to fight, and a time to retreat. For brotherhood and survival, remember Bobby. It could be your husband, your son, or your brother tomorrow. Crimes against an individual are often crimes against an entire nation. To his family: only time can eliminate the pain of losing him, but may he be remembered in the hearts and minds of all of us. Betty Shabazz.

Whatever path we seem to take, it always has one end: a racist bullet. A racist bullet murdered Malcolm X, murdered Martin Luther King, murdered Bobby Hutton. Attempted to murder Huey Newton; attempted to murder Eldridge Cleaver. From the streets, from the flying of this bullet in the air into the flesh of a black man, a whole structure proceeds: walls of courthouses, bars of jails, locked keys, billy-clubs, police.

Everywhere you turn you're encaged. The same police force, the very same police force that murdered Bobby Hutton in cold blood, deliberately, provided a funeral escort to the cemetery. The very same police force that attempted to assassinate Eldridge Cleaver is lining the highways from here to Vacaville, stacked deep. The town of Vacaville is closed down. There's double security on the penitentiary. Machine gun guards in the church.

One bullet in the flesh is not enough; 50 policemen in the streets of West Oakland is not enough for them. Right over there in the parking lot they've got 700 policemen, waiting.

Huey Newton—there on the 10th floor of the Alameda County Courthouse—Huey Newton held the key to liberating the black people. He stated if the racist-dog policemen do not withdraw from the black community, cease their wanton murder, and torture and brutality of black people, they will face the wrath of the armed people.

For the simple demand—basic human liberty—Huey Newton is in jail, charged with murder. Bobby Hutton is dead. Eldridge Cleaver is in jail, charged with three counts of assault with attempt to murder. David Hilliard, national captain of the party is in jail, three counts of murder. And a series of other brothers in the Black

Panther Party. This is only the first. They move against every leadership as it extends itself. As each group of leaders rises up their [*inaudible*], but they cannot stop [us] by wiping away our leaders. For every leader that's shot down, more spring up, until the people rise up as one man and fight and gain their liberation, and this is what this one man, Bobby Hutton, died for.

We lost something very precious when we lost Bobby Hutton. But Bobby Hutton didn't lose anything. Bobby Hutton took his stand; he gave his life. And here we are, we have our lives. He added something to them. It's up to us, to whether we can treasure that and carry that forward, or if we'll allow the walls of the jails and bullets of the racist dog police to increasingly intimidate and encircle and murder us until we degenerate into a state maintained purely by brute police power. This time, this day, is not far off. We have very little time. We are in a race against time.

Huey Newton, Eldridge Cleaver and Bobby Hutton. Thank you.

26

Barbara Lee

1946-

Congresswoman Barbara Lee, like her mentor Shirley Chisholm, is "unbought and unbossed." Courage, compassion, authenticity, and purpose define her. She was the only member of the U.S. Congress to vote against the war on Iraq following the 9/11 attacks (in which Iraq was not involved). She opposes endless war and has a social justice agenda that includes ending poverty.

Beyond Iraq, Beyond Haiti, and Beyond the Doctrine of Preemption: Once Again It Is Time to Break the Silence

Keynote address, United New York Black Radical Congress 2nd Annual Celebration of the Life of MLK: "A Festival of Dissent," April 4, 2004, Riverside Church, New York, New York

I want to thank you for that kind introduction, and I want to thank you so much for inviting me here, on this very special day, to this very special place.

I want to thank Reverend James Forbes, senior pastor here at the Riverside Church, for opening up his house of worship to this gathering and celebration in honor of the life of our great apostle for peace and prophet for liberty and justice for all, Dr. Martin Luther King, Jr.

I also want to salute the Black Radical Congress and acknowledge the work of Professor Manning Marable, a great scholar whose insights continue to clarify the moment.

Finally, I want to recognize Councilman Bill Perkins and especially my friend and colleague, Congressman Charlie Rangel, who has long been a champion for social justice and a warrior for peace in New York and in Washington, and who has raised his unmistakable voice in support of the cause of freedom and human dignity from every podium, pulpit, or soapbox in between.

I am indeed humbled to be with you this evening. I am reminded of the history of this great sanctuary and stand in awe of the life and work of the members and friends of Riverside.

In reflecting on tonight, I remembered that while working for a great statesman and warrior, Congressman Ron Dellums, I participated in an African National Congress anti-apartheid conference here at Riverside, in 1977 or 1978.

Ron could not attend and asked if I'd speak in his absence.

Knowing how sacred and special this church is, I was, of course, quite nervous.

Well, nothing has changed. It's more than a quarter of a century later, but I'm still just as nervous.

To stand in this spot, in the pulpit where our great prince of peace and prophet Dr. King stood 37 years ago, is a life defining and life affirming moment for me. For that I am deeply grateful.

On this day in 1967, Dr. King delivered his famous address, "Beyond Vietnam: A Time to Break Silence."

On that day in 1967, he began, "I come to this magnificent house of worship tonight because my conscience leaves me no choice." He was compelled to speak, he said, because "A time comes when silence is betrayal."

In confronting the war in Vietnam, Dr. King was challenging not only the administration in power, but also many members of the civil rights community, a challenge that he explained in his Riverside address.

"Over the past two years," he said, "as I have moved to break the betrayal of my own silences and to speak from the burnings of my own heart, as I have called for radical departures from the destruction of Vietnam, many persons have questioned me about the wisdom of my path. At the heart of their concerns this query has often loomed large and loud: Why are you speaking about war, Dr. King? Why are you joining the voices of dissent?

"Peace and civil rights don't mix, they say. Aren't you hurting the cause of your people, they ask? And when I hear them, though I often understand the source of their concern, I am nevertheless greatly saddened, for such questions mean that the inquirers have not really known me, my commitment or my calling. Indeed, their questions suggest that they do not know the world in which they live."

On April 4th, 1967, Dr. King spelled out very clearly the connections and costs between war abroad and the price paid here at home. And his words are as true today as they were almost four decades ago.

He said, "I knew that America would never invest the necessary funds or energies in rehabilitation of its poor so long as adventures like Vietnam continued to draw men and skills and money like some demonic destructive suction tube. So I was increasingly compelled to see the war as an enemy of the poor and to attack it as such."

Dr. King then went on to list a number of other reasons for his opposition to the war.

The war in Vietnam, he explained, was exacting an extraordinarily high price among young black men.

It was also undermining the ability of the United States to act as a force for non-violence either at home or abroad.

And, it was poisoning our national soul and the nation's spiritual values, which, as a Christian, Dr. King said that he had to speak out against.

Finally, Dr. King said, the Vietnamese people who were the victims of so much violence and destruction must see Americans as very "strange liberators."

I wanted to take the time to read so much of Dr. King's speech both because of the power of his words in 1967 and because of the power and richness of their resonance today.

I'd like to talk about that resonance in terms of the Bush Administration's foreign policy.

Specifically, I would like to talk about the coup in Haiti and the war in Iraq, but I'd also like to talk about the policies that extend from them, just as Dr. King looked beyond the war in Vietnam and into our very national soul.

When we look beyond these countries what we see is a much broader, more sweeping foreign policy that is making the world a more dangerous place. Haiti and Iraq are manifestations of the Bush foreign policy as a whole.

And Americans are still very "strange liberators," as Dr. King said, liberators who sow resentment rather than relief.

In the last few weeks in Haiti we witnessed the overthrow of a democratically elected government off our own shores.

The overthrow of the Aristide government did not suddenly take place on one Sunday in February. It was a process that took years.

As co-chair of the Congressional Black Caucus Haiti Task Force, I saw what was happening and tried to sound the alarm.

For years the Bush Administration did everything in its power to cut off international economic assistance to Haiti, the poorest country in this hemisphere.

The Congressional Black Caucus refused to stand idly by and let this happen, and we finally forced the release of loans from international financial institutions.

But the damage to Haiti's opportunity to foster economic development had already been done.

Then, having helped strangle Haiti economically, the Bush Administration did nothing as internal violence rose in that country, threatening the democratically elected Aristide government.

Article 17 of the Inter-American Democratic Charter of the Organization of American States requires that all OAS nations come to the aid of a democratic government under siege.

But in Haiti, the Bush Administration did not come to Haiti's aid. Instead it resisted efforts in the UN to organize a peace-keeping mission to create the time, space, and security on the ground that was needed for a democratic resolution.

Next the Administration publicly abandoned President Aristide and then pressured him to leave.

Make no mistake, the United States helped overthrow a duly elected president by accelerating and assisting a coup d'etat in Haiti.

They helped force Haiti's only democratically elected president in history out of office and into exile.

We did send in the Marines—but only after we had helped oust democracy from the country.

This was regime change—not by outright invasion, but first by indifference and then by intervention.

First the Administration undermined democracy, then they helped destroy it.

In the process, they trampled the UN Charter, the OAS Charter, and our own principles, ideals, and credibility.

Dr. Jeffrey Sachs, a professor at Columbia and an adviser to UN Secretary General Kofi Annan, has stated that the Bush foreign policy team came into office determined to topple Aristide and then set about making it happen.

Is this beginning to sound familiar?

I'll tell you this—there are a lot of familiar faces involved: Roger Noriega, is the Assistant Secretary of State for Western Hemisphere Affairs and is considered the mastermind of the Bush Administration's Haiti policy. Back in the Reagan days he worked in the State Department to help overthrow the Nicaraguan government.

He is joined by Otto Reich, Special Representative for Hemispheric Initiatives, another Iran-Contra veteran; and John Negroponte, now U.S. Ambassador to the UN, who was also deeply involved in Iran-Contra and tied to human rights violations in Latin America.

You add these Reagan veterans to the younger generation in the

White House who preach preemption and war rather than cooperation and law, and you get an incredibly dangerous agenda.

That is why I have sponsored HR 3919, the TRUTH Act: a bill to create an independent commission to investigate the role of the United States government in the overthrow of the Aristide government and the destruction of the democratic process in that country. We must demand an investigation.

Tonight I am asking every one of you to help me with this bill.

I want you to go home and call or email your congressman or woman and ask them to cosponsor this bill. But you can let Charlie Rangel off the hook—he's already a cosponsor!

We have to do this because we all know that Haiti is neither the beginning nor the end of the Bush Administration's assault on democracy.

Once again, having toppled a government, the Bush Administration has helped unleash waves of looting, destruction, and havoc that it apparently failed to plan for.

And it has neglected the humanitarian and development needs of the Haitian people. Again, I have to ask, does this sound familiar?

Just how many governments does this Administration plan to overthrow? That question brings me to my second topic today: the war in Iraq.

The war in Iraq and the overthrow of the Aristide government in Haiti are both products of a foreign policy that is based on unilateralism rather than international cooperation, that is short-sighted rather than visionary, and that is based on principles of preemption rather than engagement and international law.

Last month marked the one year anniversary of the beginning of the war in Iraq, a war that continues to take American and Iraqi lives.

Congress marked this anniversary by passing a resolution that celebrated the war but completely ignored its causes, costs, and consequences.

This resolution stated that the war in Iraq had made the world a safer place. I could not disagree more.

This resolution is one more lie, one more link in a chain of deception and distortion. This resolution never mentioned the almost 600 Americans and unknown numbers of Iraqis who have died.

It never mentioned the $165 billion that this war has already sucked out of our national treasury.

It never mentioned the invisible weapons of mass destruction that supposedly were the reason for fighting this war.

And it never mentioned what this war has cost us in terms of international credibility, our domestic priorities, or our national security.

Those are lies of omission.

I offered an amendment to this warped resolution that would have acknowledged the casualties and costs of this war and the fact that it has made the world more dangerous, not more secure.

The Republican leadership refused to even allow my amendment to come up for a vote: that is one more way they have sought to silence dissent.

The Republicans in Congress and the White House first sought to silence debate and demonize the opposition with the Patriot Act and the resolutions against Afghanistan and Iraq, and they continue to do so today by attacking the patriotism and commitment to national security of any of their opponents.

But we will not be silenced. We will not sit idly by while they do this to our country.

The Book of Ephesians, Chapter 6, Verse 10, teaches us to "put on the full armor of God, so that when the day of evil comes, you may be able to stand your ground, and after you have done everything, to stand."

That's asking a lot of you. It's no easy task, but it's what Ephesians asks.

The Scripture continues, "Stand firm then, with the belt of truth buckled around your waist, with breastplate of righteousness in place, and with your feet fitted with the readiness that comes from the gospel of peace."

That's what I ask you to do today, to stand firmly, and after you have done everything, in the face of all the pressure we confront, we still must stand.

Dr. King was a prophet of the gospel of peace. He left us both a message and a mission to follow, and in his honor, and in upholding his legacy, we must challenge the Administration's foreign and domestic policies and demand peace with justice.

Remember, Dr. King said that peace was not just the absence of tension but the presence of justice.

For me personally, Dr. King's message was uppermost in my mind on September 14th, 2001, when just three days after a terrible, heartbreaking shock, Congress rushed in anger, anguish, and grief to pass a resolution unleashing unlimited force against unknown enemies.

I didn't know I would be alone in my vote that day, but, as the Scriptures say, I knew that I had to stand.

I could not vote to give the Administration a blank check to wage war, I could not vote, and I quote here from the language of the resolution, to authorize the President "to use all necessary and appropriate force against those nations, organizations, or persons he determines planned, authorized, committed, or aided the terrorist attacks that occurred on September 11, 2001, or harbored such organizations or persons."

As I said that fall, this "was a blank check to the President to attack anyone involved in the September 11th events—anywhere, in any country, without regard to our nation's long-term foreign policy, economic and national security interests, and without time limit. In granting these overly broad powers, Congress failed its responsibility to understand the dimensions of its declaration.

"I could not support such a grant of war-making authority. I believe it would put more innocent lives at risk. We must respond but the character of that response will determine for us and our children the world that they will inherit.

"I do not dispute the President's intent to rid the world of terrorism, but we have many means to reach that goal, and measures that spawn further acts of terror or that do not address the sources of hatred do not increase our security."

In measuring the tremendous loss of the victims of 9-11 and pondering the response, I drew on the wisdom of a clergy man who spoke that day at the National Cathedral: "Let us not become the evil that we deplore."

With those words ringing in my ears, I could not vote for unrestrained war.

Dr. King's voice was also with me in the fall of 2002 when Congress gave the Bush Administration a second blank check to wage war against Iraq.

It is a message that is with me when I fight against the Administration's efforts to undermine democracy in Haiti, when I struggle against its determination to underfund money for HIV-AIDS, and when I battle against this President's neglect of our nation's terrible needs for housing, healthcare, and jobs.

It is not enough to simply be against the war or against the Administration. We must also be *for* something.

That is why in the fall of 2002 when Congress was debating the resolution authorizing force against Iraq, I offered an amendment that spelled out another path, a path of expanded UN inspections and sustained engagement.

The inspections process was working. We did not need to go to war.

My amendment, which received 72 votes, would have avoided this entire war.

My amendment grew out of a larger progressive foreign policy strategy that runs directly counter to the perilous unilateralism of the Bush Administration's Doctrine of Preemption, which we have already seen at work in Iraq.

As a progressive, I also support the principles of smart security that are embodied in a bill recently introduced by my friend and colleague, Congresswoman Lynn Woolsey of California. This is a bill that I hope you embrace.

Smart security would help us rebuild alliances and defuse rather than initiate conflict.

This approach would make real strides toward reducing nuclear stockpiles and curbing the proliferation of weapons of mass destruction and would help us cut off the financial resources of terrorists to keep deadly weapons out of their hands.

Finally, smart security would also mean smart defense spending that would enhance homeland security, invest in energy security, and eliminate the Cold War military industrial complex that is still alive and well.

Smart security would let us redirect resources to where we need them most. As Dr. King taught us, "A nation that continues year after year to spend more on military defense than on programs of social uplift is approaching spiritual death."

I also ask you to rally support for this bill, H. Con. Res. 392. It provides a better way, a way that I'm certain Dr. King would embrace.

When Dr. King asked the congregation gathered in this holy place in 1967 to look beyond Vietnam, he was asking them both to oppose that war and to support policies and principles of peace and justice at home and abroad.

I ask you to do the same thing today. I ask you to organize and mobilize, to stand up against the forces of both silence and oppression.

We can take back this country by taking back the White House—remember, regime change begins at home!

And we can take back the House of Representatives so that Charlie Rangel is no longer just the ranking minority member of the powerful Ways and Means Committee but instead is its chairman.

Then we'll see our resources going for building schools, not prisons; for jobs not tax cuts for the wealthy; for building affordable housing not bombs; and for creating a universal health care system instead of enriching the insurance industry.

It is our charge to take up this challenge, as persons of faith, as believers in justice.

I leave you now again with the words of Dr. King when he spoke from this pulpit in 1967, as he stood firm on behalf of the gospel of peace, as he asked those gathered here to look beyond Vietnam.

He said, "If we do not act we shall surely be dragged down the long dark and shameful corridors of time reserved for those who possess power without compassion, might without morality, and strength without sight."

In closing, let me just reiterate, ours cannot be a nation of compassionless power, immoral might, or blind strength.

We must be better than that. Dr. King would demand that we be better than that.

As he said, "The choice is ours, and though we might prefer it otherwise, we must choose in this crucial moment of human history."

So we must work each and every day for regime change in Washington, DC. We must take up Dr. King's charge not as a burden but as a privileged legacy.

Riverside Church has been the scene of so many great moments. I ask all of you to make this evening one more milestone in that tremendous pageant.

Because you are the ones who can and will make the difference, who can and will take us forward into the light of a better day.

Thank you for all that you do, and thank you again for allowing me to speak to you on this special day, on this hallowed ground.

27

Carol Moseley Braun

1947-

Elected to the U.S. Senate in 1993, Carol Moseley Braun was the first Black woman in American history to hold this position—and only the second African American senator to be elected since Reconstruction. She served a single term in office, representing the state of Illinois; while in office she championed issues relating to health care, education, and civil rights. In 1999, President Bill Clinton appointed her as U.S. ambassador to New Zealand, a post she held for two years. When she was sworn in as a U.S. senator, Moseley Braun remarked that "I cannot escape the fact that I come to the Senate as a symbol of hope and change. Nor would I want to, because my presence in and of itself will change the U.S. Senate."

Announcement Speech for Democratic Nomination

Howard University, September 22, 2003, Washington, DC

I would like to thank Howard University for opening these historic halls to us today, and for affording us the opportunity to take this step on such solid ground in the tradition of excellence that Howard exemplifies.

I would like to thank each and every one of you for taking time to share this moment. I am encouraged and inspired by you, and confident in the knowledge that our democracy is safe so long as young people know that it is not a spectator sport.

I would like to thank the National Organization for Women and the National Women's Political Caucus for their endorsements. Their clarity and advocacy for women gives me the hope and the support I must have to engage in this effort.

I would like to thank all of the friends, supporters, and strangers, too, who have led me along my path towards this day. Over the past several months I have traveled America, talking with people, listening to them, registering voters and engaging in a passionate debate about our country's direction. I am grateful to all those who opened their homes and their hearts, to those who shared their experiences with me, and who made it possible for me to explore the prospect of a presidential campaign. Thank you for your encouragement.

Today, I am officially declaring my candidacy for the Democratic nomination for President of the United States.

I am running for the Democratic nomination because I believe this party ought to stand for inclusion, hope, and new ways to resolve old problems.

I am fighting for the nomination because I am determined to move our party in the direction of our nation's most noble ideals, and live up to our generation's duty to leave the next generation no less freedom, no less opportunity, no less optimism than we inherited from our ancestors.

I am dedicated to building partnerships for peace, prosperity and progress based on new ideas that are as practical as they are innovative. These partnerships will help us shape an American renaissance and renewal in the best traditions of our country.

I have the experience, the ability and the ideas to heal and renew America. In all of my public service, I have broken down barriers, built bridges and brought people together to achieve solutions that put the public interest first.

As a young federal prosecutor, I won a Justice Department award for my work to put an end to exploitation in housing policy.

As a state representative, I fought for education, and passed laws to create the first local school councils and agriculture schools in Illinois. My colleagues voted me the "Conscience of the House" for my advocacy for the poor.

As a county executive, I convened the first advisory council, and worked with organized labor to improve conditions for the employees and the public. When I left that office, it had become a profit center for Cook County, the workers were better off, and the public was better served.

As a United States Senator, and as the first woman to serve on the Finance Committee, I passed laws for women's pension equity, and for environmental remediation and alternative energy, for school modernization and restoration of the interest deduction for college loans.

As Ambassador, I was credited with improving relations on behalf of the United States, and was the first envoy to be made an honorary member of the Te Atiawa Maori tribe.

Breaking barriers; building bridges; bringing people together: I have been blessed to be an agent for change and progress, but I cannot take full personal credit for these accomplishments. I have always depended on the help and support of people of good will who had the vision to imagine the possibilities borne of giving me a chance to contribute.

I tell the people what I believe in, I keep my promises and I hold myself accountable for my service. My entire public life has been characterized by problem solving with new ideas that are as practical as they are innovative. I want to bring my skills and my experience to bear on healing our country, and creating a renaissance for America.

Through partnerships for peace and prosperity and progress we will renew the American dream of freedom and opportunity.

We can make our economy work for everyone, not just the already wealthy, and assure families that they will be able to provide decent housing, health care, education, retirement and safety to those they love the most.

We will turn away from the bluster and bravado that has so soured our friendships and alliances around the world, and build our global relationships.

We will respect individuals in their private lives, in their professional endeavors and in their civic engagements.

And we will tap all of the talent that is available to us, without limitation of any aspect of personality that serves to divide instead of glorify the human condition.

America will be stronger when we engage the full range of talent that is at our disposal, and when we live up to our most fundamental national virtues.

We can, and must renew the American spirit. What makes this country great is not the size of its military or its budget or its wealth, but the spirit of her people. That spirit has been battered since 9/11; not only by the criminals who killed so many, but by leaders who have pandered to fear in its aftermath. We must not allow the nightmare of our limitations to continue; but instead dream a world of the best of who we are.

When we come together to create partnerships for peace and prosperity and progress we will heal the American spirit.

Partnerships for peace will bring a real end to this Iraqi war, and bring our troops home with honor. Americans don't cut and run, and so we have to see this misadventure through to a noble conclusion. The sacrifice of those who lost their lives in the sands of Iraq will not be forgotten, but neither will the folly of preemptive war.

Partnerships for peace will build on the goodwill that we had after 9/11, and engage our allies to help us leave Iraq better than we found it.

Partnerships for peace will give our international institutions new support for global collaborations to fight crime and terrorism, poverty and disease. Our foreign policy will follow our values, and serve the interests of the American people.

Trade can create opportunity to share our values, not lose our jobs. We can engage our private sector in ways that will bolster their bottom line, stem job hemorrhage at home and help stop the exploitation of workers and the environment around the world. I want to forge partnerships for prosperity that will explore new policies to stop our nation's slide toward embedded wealth, entrenched poverty, and a shrinking middle class.

When we pursue balance in our economic order, we will embrace fiscal, monetary and trade policies that put working people first. Economic policy is so interconnected with our nation's social fabric that government has a special duty to protect the people from the forces of private interest and greed.

I believe in fiscal responsibility and fighting for social justice. Partnerships for prosperity give us opportunity to do good and do well simultaneously. We will fight the greedy—whose excesses and crimes have threatened our capital markets and undermined confidence in our economy. We will help the needy—whether in childhood or retirement, in sickness or despair.

Achieving a balanced budget again will help restore confidence in our policymakers' ability to protect our nation's economic health. This administration has no right to make irresponsible spending decisions that simply shift the payment burden onto those least able to pay, or to state and local governments, or, worse still, to our children and grandchildren.

Without spending a dime more than we already pay, we can provide health security that emphasizes wellness, restores the provider/patient relationship and maintains the quality of care Americans have every right to expect. Embracing a single payer system of health insurance that does not depend on employment will not only provide universal coverage, but boost our international competitiveness, stimulate our economy at home, and let workers keep more of their pay.

Education reform that relieves the burden on local property taxpayers, while empowering parents and teachers to pursue excellence and innovation is an opportunity for a partnership for prosperity that we cannot afford to ignore if we are to keep our country strong. The cornerstone of the American dream of opportunity is education—it is the way our workforce is prepared to engage the rest of the world. Education is not just a private benefit, but a public good as well, and our national interest is bound up in providing quality public education for every child.

We can engage in partnerships for prosperity to build infrastructure, as well. Especially in the wake of the recent events, storms and blackouts and other calamities, we all know that our foundations—for energy, for water, for transportation—are in need of restoration. By bringing together national, state and local governments with the private sector, including colleges and universities and non-governmental organizations, we can spark a building boom that will unleash innovation and technology transfers and create new industries and new wealth. Private industry will give us the benefit of the best America has to offer, and when we make government a partner in our country's renovation, we will create jobs and opportunity and hope for all Americans.

As President, I will give you an America as good as its promise. I will reach out to bring us together to create an American renaissance, revival and renewal. I am uniquely qualified to do the job of President, and I offer the clearest alternative to this current administration, whose only new idea has been preemptive war and a huge new bureaucracy. I can fix the mess they have created, because I am practical, I am not afraid of partnerships and I am committed to making the world better for our children. By tapping the talent, the ideas, and the capacity that our whole society has to offer, we will expand the probability of succeeding together.

America is at a tipping point; if we stay the course we are on, we won't recognize this country 5 years from now. But if we shift gears, try another way, tap some of the talent that has been relegated to the sidelines of leadership, we can heal and renew and save our country.

Just last week, my little 9-year-old niece Claire called me into her room to show me her social studies book. Turning to the pages on which all of our Presidents were pictured, she looked at me and complained: But Auntie Carol, all the Presidents are boys!

I want Claire, and your daughters and sons to know that in America, everyone has a chance to serve and contribute. I believe that America is ready to take the next great step in the direction of her most noble ideals of service and merit and equality.

This campaign is our way of fighting to give Claire and every American girl or boy not only the opportunity to become President of this great country, but the freedom to decide to lead a quality private life if they choose to do so. There is no human power greater than a made up mind, and we have decided not to let them take away our liberty, our opportunity, our hope for a better future.

The time has come to meet the challenge of our founding fathers' vision, and I am prepared to fight for you and with you to revive the American dream of freedom and opportunity. Together we will break down barriers.

Together we will rebuild and restore our country. And together we will give ourselves the greatest gift of all: an America we can be proud of.

Thank you for your patriotism. Thank you for your energy. Thank you for your faith in the goodness of this country. We will lift up the hearts of the American people. We will inspire hope. We will renew the American Spirit. And we will win. Together, failure is impossible.

28

Ruby Nell Sales

1948-

As a young voting rights activist in 1965, Ruby Sales left the Tuskegee Institute to devote herself full time to the epic struggle to bring democracy to the South. That summer, she was jailed in Lowndes County, Alabama (known as "Bloody Lowndes" for its history of violence), along with a group of fellow activists. On her release, when she tried to enter a local store to get something to drink, a local sheriff's deputy threatened her with a loaded shotgun. A white seminarian named Jonathan Daniels stepped in to protect her; the deputy killed Daniels with a single shotgun blast. Traumatized, Sales was unable to speak for months, but she recovered—and committed herself to a life of passionate activism on behalf of equality and civil rights.

Can I Get a Witness?

St. John the Divine Cathedral, September 10, 2017,
Episcopal Diocese of New York, New York

By and by when the morning comes
When all the Saints of God gather home
We will tell the story of how we overcome
And we will understand it better by and by.
—Black spiritual

Amen.

You may be seated.

Good morning, God's people. I would like to thank the Right Rev. Clifton Daniel for his generous invitation for me to worship with you this morning in the community of St. John the Divine. My thankfulness goes out to Reverend Cannon Patrick Malloy and Reverend Mary Julia Jett for their assistance in making this day possible. I am filled with humility for the opportunity to deepen our faith and theology together in this time of both great desolation and fertile possibilities to "redeem the soul of Christianity and

America." For this opportunity and gift, "my soul doth magnify the Lord."

I come to you this morning in this magnificent Cathedral on the heels of this church's 52nd celebration of the witness of our honored one, Jonathan Daniels, who in the flicker of an eye without hesitation mightily gave evidence of his faith by giving up his life to save mine. Yet despite our rituals of celebration, far too many Christians remain glued to our seats seduced by the opiates of the Empire. These opiates numb us to the same suffering and systemic rot that moved Jonathan to get up from the King's table and journey to a strange land among Black peasants and young freedom fighters to become one with God's mandate to let God's kingdom come on earth as it is in heaven.

Yet despite Christians who celebrate and claim Jon's witness as their own, far too many of us as church leaders become blinded by our Empire gaze and our adoration of all its entitlements. We strut in front of ordinary people in our academic gowns and demand the best seats in the house. I come to you this morning when all around the globe in countries of color everywhere the guardians of White male supremacy have torn up communities of color and gobbled up their resources and made them poor, homeless and hungry. There are millions of children of color around the globe living in the streets homeless because we have destroyed their homes. Yet, when they come to our door seeking refuge and reparations for the harm we have done, many White Americans distance themselves from these immigrant survivors with hard and cold hearts that interfere with their ability to see our sister and brother immigrants of color as being fully human.

Because of this, we do not believe that they deserve the same opportunities that we destroyed for them in their countries. The guardians of White supremacy wrap themselves in self-righteous rhetoric that allows them to justify and ignore the homelessness and spiritual warfare that resulted from this country's foreign policies that destroyed the inner and outer infrastructures in communities of color.

Further, I come to you this morning as churches throughout cities in this country remain silent at the predatory action of the real estate industrial complex that cleanses the city of people of color, poor and middle class people. Under this new world order of a capitalist technocracy most people are unessential and disposable waste, especially people of color, women, seniors and children.

Despite the fact that New York is the financial heartbeat of this new world order, members of the church harden their hearts to the homelessness and despair of God's people who have been forced to become wanderers and exiles from communities that they worked hard to build. Yet, it doesn't end here. Churches throw their lot in with real estate developers by selling their property to the highest bidder and fertilizing this rapacious system that kicks ordinary working people out of cities into rural sites of isolation without access to jobs, services or decent education for children.

I predict that in the 21st century these sites of isolation will become Bantu communities similar to the ones in South Africa in the 20th century as well as sites of White violence against people of color who will compete with them for the meager resources that exist in these rural communities.

Sisters and brothers, this morning I tell you that we are sitting on a powder keg, and the church is participating in lighting the fire. I cannot help but remember the quote, "And God saw the rainbow sign—No more water but the fire next time."

With all these rumblings and meditations in my heart, I come to you as a remnant who lived during segregation when Pharaoh's and his people's hearts were hard with the bricks of Southern Apartheid and state sanctioned terror against my people. As a child, I heard the cries of my people as they witnessed Emmitt Till's battered, adolescent body broken and lynched by White supremacists who did not see him as a child but saw him as an enemy combatant who threatened their way of life and who must be destroyed.

I read the accounts of Mary Turner, a young pregnant Black female who was lynched by White vigilantes who cut her fetus out of her body and smashed it against the ground and then burned her body alive. I heard my people's cry and petition to God, "How long, how long, oh God, how long must we suffer and how much must we endure?"

God heard our cry. As a remnant, I participated in that Kairos moment in the Southern freedom struggle where I saw ordinary people of all colors in this country move from the low level of an Empire consciousness to a mountaintop consciousness where they imagined a world house and a Pentacost moment and went all the way to achieve it.

It was in this movement moment that I witnessed miracles of faith born out of Black folk theology that instilled Black children to stand up and not be afraid as police unleashed on them water hoses with water moving at a speed of 180 miles an hour as well as big German Shepherd dogs that clutched at their little throats. It was in this moment of mountaintop consciousness that in a Mississippi jail where White jailers beat Annelle Ponder, a young Black female freedom fighter, until her body was broken and demanded that she call them "Sir" that she raised her hands in defiance and muttered the words through bruised lips, "Freedom now, freedom now."

During this moment of mountaintop consciousness, I saw ordinary Black people move into action and confront the powers and principalities of Southern Apartheid and White Supremacy in the streets marching and singing, "Ain't gonna let nobody turn me around. Gonna keep on walking, gonna keep on talking, gonna keep on marching up freedom's highway." In this season, God lifted me up and gave me, a 17-year-old Southern Black girl, the least of all of them, a new name, a new consciousness and a new status. It was Freedom Fighter.

Having witnessed all of this, I saw us turn in another direction in the highway and go from the mountaintop to the arid desert and the wilderness years where we forgot who had been our Benefactor and we knelt down at the altar of the very Empire of which we had fought to be free. My soul wept as I witnessed us in this wilderness commit the idolatry of worshipping at the altar of Whiteness rather than bow down at the altar of God who had brought us a mighty long way out of the dreary land of oppression to the bright promise of a freedom land.

I saw in these desert years my White brothers and sisters once again closing the door on another opportunity to remove the cataracts of oppression from their eyes that would give them a clear vision straight to the Kingdom of God.

As a witness and a remnant of this time standing in the fertile ground of three scores and ten, I bring to this gathering this morning and to the reading of the text God's merciful grace of hindsight, insight and foresight. For all these corners in my life in which I have stood, my soul does magnify the Lord.

Even as I offer this testimony and thanksgiving this morning, I must confess that I struggled with the question of how to speak firmly about the leaks in the church while holding out the grace, love and mercy that are pathways for our redemption.

The text often seemed irreconcilable to a theological praxis of God's love, grace and mercy as I wrestled with words such as confrontation, moral accountability, God's wrath and punishment, and God's grace and mercy. Both in the Hebrew Scripture and in the Gospel, we meet a God of wrath and one who pushes us to confront those who trespass against us personally and systemically.

Christians, especially White ones, are apt to hold up God's love rather than God's wrath, God's mercy rather than God's judgment because often they have learned from the Empire that they are beloved no matter how they treat others and that they are above accountability, even to God.

Despite what appears to be major contradictions in the text, from the outside it is clear that God is on the side of those who confront their wrong doers. Not only is God on the side of those of us who confront our wrong doers, but God demands and requires it. If the wrong doers refuse to hear, God intervenes in human history to set right the wrongs that our trespassers refuse to change.

Before I move forward with what is obvious, let me clear up the discordant notes that appear to be in the text. Forgiveness is not antithetical to punishment, judgment or accountability. Both the Hebrew text and the Gospel this morning remind us that although God is a forgiving God this does not mean that God does not hold us accountable for our wrong doings and does not judge us for our obstinate refusal to do towards others what we know is right. Because God is merciful, God gives us the opportunity to make amends and repair the harm to others.

To think that God does not hold us accountable for our wrong doings or our sins is to arrogantly mock God and suggest that God is a God who condones systemic and personal evil. As I understand the text, forgiveness is God's grace, mercy and active love that guarantee we are not captives of history and that we can change the world that we helped to create and in which we live.

For the instigators or practitioners of systemic injustice in this country, whether they are White supremacists or misogynists, God provides them with many open doors to break with the culture of oppression and begin anew. As much as they desire it, God does not give them a free pass to commit the same violations over and over again without accountability and consequences. God's love does not give us easy grace. Rather, it gives us the agency to do the hard work of justice.

The Scripture tells us this morning that our first step in confronting wrongdoing, in this case White supremacy and all of its oppressive tributaries such as misogyny, is to go directly to the wrongdoers and point it out. I think I can say without hesitation that Black and Brown people have adhered to this requirement. For we have consistently spoken plainly to the male guardians of White supremacy and their adherents. We have told them in the words of my ancestors how they treat us. We've marched, we've sat in, we've laid our cases before presidents, and yet, the White Supremacists' hearts remain unmoved, hard and brittle and their mouths drip with ideologies that give rise to perverse policies.

This includes leaders of God's church who strangle truth every Sunday with the lie of a White Jesus and a liturgy filled with White Empire symbols and anti-Black and Brown language. It is hard to get through to a church that associates the crucifixion of Jesus by state sanctioned murderers as the high point in his story rather than the incredible, compassionate life that Jesus led committed to justice, love and reconciliation. Or they continue to perpetuate a Constantinian and Empire view of Christianity that links the cross with Empire building, invasion, captivity, dispersion and spiritual warfare. These are the leaks in the Church that numb its leaders and members to suffering, injustice and state sanctioned violence.

The Scripture tells us that the next step is to gather witnesses to go with us to present our case so that every word may be confirmed by their evidence. Black and Brown people have gathered witnesses throughout the years who have gone with us to the Supreme Court, to Congress, to houses of worship and to the streets of America to bear witness and offer evidence of the pernicious and devastating presence of White supremacy not only on Black people but also on every life that it touches.

It is in the spirit of this text that I come to you this morning and ask you to bear witness with me as I share with you what I believe and understand to be the deep troubling in this land.

White America faces a spiritual crisis of meaning and identity that gets to the very heart of what kind of people will they become in the 21st century. There is an insatiable appetite in the White west that has yet to be filled.

As I watch the land grab in the cities of the real estate industrial complex, it strikes me that there is an insatiable hunger in the White western soul for materialism or the materialization of power. This hunger feeds a historical narrative of greed, land theft, the devouring of natural resources and creatures, genocide, White patriarchal Christian imperialism, cultural plunder of colored communities, space exploration, and all forms of social oppression.

Yet, the spoils from all of these are not enough because the hunger is a spiritual one that cannot be satisfied with materialism. It is an emptiness of the Spirit that has plagued the entire globe. It has become the essence of the spiritual and social identity of Whiteness and White male supremacy.

Until the White west addresses this crisis, all the work for social justice will not yield core or sustainable changes. Our brothers and witnesses, Martin Luther King Jr. and Vincent Harding, knew this when they told us that nothing less than a "Revolution of values" would fill up the spiritual emptiness of the West that gives rise to militarism, materialism and racism.

The call for the 21st century for the White west and all of us who have been socialized with these perverse and insatiable hungers is a spiritual one that changes the soul of the west.

Everywhere I look, this hunger precipitates suffering in God's people. I ask you this morning, do you have eyes to see, a heart to feel and ears to hear? I ask you, is there a balm in Gilead? If so, where is it? And how might we lubricate our spirits to heal our sin sick and assaulted souls? Are there spiritual doctors in the land and in God's house who can write a theological prescription that raises the people of God up from our beds of affliction and disposability so that we might walk again?

I want to know this morning is there a people fashioning a living theology out of our dry bones that will give new and powerful meaning to our lives. I want to know this morning, brothers and sisters, can the church turn sights of desolation into hope zones?

This is the work that we must all do. It is not work that White Americans do for other people but work they must do for themselves. It is spiritual work that redeems my White sisters and brothers from a death driven culture that diminishes their humanity and creates in them chronic fear of others that makes it impossible to live on the land in relationship to other people without seeking containment sites such as segregated housing, communities and schools. It is a death driven system that lacks faith and hope and breeds cynicism that sabotages the democracy and goodness that reside in my White sisters and brothers.

Even as I come to confront powers and principalities this morning, I come with a hope that is borne out of the historical documentation of White people throughout the history of this country who have broken with Empire culture, whether in the Abolitionist, Labor, Peace, Southern Freedom, Northern Freedom and Gender Rights Movements.

I am filled with hope because of God's grace and mercy that do not hold us as hostages to bad history. Despite the stranglehold of all forms of Empire oppression, we have the power to wrestle free and breathe new life into Democracy and Christianity.

To all my brothers and sisters, this is the day to rejoice because this is our season to replenish the earth with a just and loving way forward recognizing that for generations White men had the mantel and they bent it towards injustice, hatred, and militarism.

Yes this is our time to do it differently by not isolating or dismissing them but by recognizing their capacity to become new people and by calling them into a new way of being that provides a balm for the woundedness of the spiritual malformation of White supremacy. This is our time to model a new and compassionate world that harmonizes the I with the We. Let us seize it with hope and commitment to erase the Empire within it even as we erase it in the world.

This is the day that the Lord has made. Let us rejoice in the open door that God in God's untiring mercy swings wide for us to build a movement of redemption and restoration where we move nonviolently from fragmentation into a wholeness of ourselves and community.

Church, this is our world and not the Empire's. We are the children of God and beneficiaries of God's creation. Let us nurture and attend to our gift.

Even as we wrestle with the desolation before us, let us not give into despair, cynicism and ingratitude. Let us thank God for another day to go forward with the spirit of justice, hospitality and reconciliation in our hearts and actions. Can I get a witness that God's mercy is everlasting?

This is what the writer of Amazing Grace realized when he wrote the words, "Amazing Grace, how sweet the sound that saved a wretch like me. I once was lost but now I'm found, was blind but now I see."

Thanks be to God and Amen.

ACKNOWLEDGMENTS

To Diane Wachtell, executive director, and Tara Grove, former editorial director, at The New Press, who suggested that the time was now for a book of speeches by African American women. They were right, of course, and entrusted me with carrying out this wonderful endeavor—for which I am forever grateful.

Once the research began, I realized that a long view was important to illustrate the vision, the courage, the brilliance, the prophecy of Black women—who had few models and few resources, but through their fierce intellect and amazing dedication to the struggle for freedom created roads by walking.

Because of the challenges created by the pandemic, this book had a long gestation period. When Tara left The New Press, Marc Favreau became my editor and continued the incredible support and encouragement to complete this book. This book could not have been completed without him. Other essential members of the New Press team included Emily Albarillo, associate managing editor, whose patience, skill, and gentle prodding kept the book production moving along and helped create a truly beautiful book, as well as Brian Ulicky, associate publisher, and Emily Janakiram, publicist.

This book owes much to Renee Floyd Myers, who was the primary researcher and who helped compile the manuscript. I am immensely thankful for her dedication, commitment, and gracious support.

Although we researched a number of sources, special acknowledgment must be given to the Carrie Chapman Catt Center for Women and Politics at Iowa State University as a source for many of the speeches.

Thank are due to Taj A. Brown who, as with *Lighting the Fires of Freedom*, has continued as my thought partner. Taj also reviewed the manuscript, and helped secure permissions.

The late artist Inge Hardison created the Sojourner Truth statue, from which we designed the front cover. Thanks to her daughter Yolande Hardison for granting us permission to use it and to photographer Richard Cabral for his wonderful cover photo and for the author's photo.

And, of course, thanks to Sir Paul McCartney for writing "Blackbird" in 1968 as a tribute to the American Civil Rights Movement. He credits the Little Rock Nine with inspiring him to write this incredibly beautiful and haunting song; I credit him with inspiring the title of this book.

PERMISSIONS

Every effort has been made to find the owners of copyright for the works included in this anthology. The editor gratefully acknowledges the following permissions and sources for the works and apologizes if any were missed. Rights holders should kindly contact info@thenewpress.com with any permissions questions.

Ella Baker, "The Black Woman in the Civil Rights Struggle," 1969. Used with permission of John Wiley & Sons.

Pauli Murray, "The Negro Woman in the Quest for Equality (Excerpts)," 1963. Reprinted with the permission of Salky Literary Management as agent for the author. Copyright © 1963 by Pauli Murray.

Dorothy I. Height, "Untitled Speech at the Opening of the Bethune Museum and Archives for Black Women," 1979. Permission from Mary McLeod Bethune Council House National Historic Site, National Archives for Black Women's History.

Margaret Walker Alexander, "Discovering Our Connections: Race, Gender, and the Law," 1992. Courtesy American University.

Gwendolyn Brooks, "Speech to the Young: Speech to the Progress-Toward (Among Them Nora and Henry III)." Reprinted by Consent of Brooks Permissions.

Fannie Lou Hamer, "I'm Sick and Tired of Being Sick and Tired," 1964. Permission from Jacqueline Hamer Flakes.

Fannie Lou Hamer, "Testimony Before the Credentials Committee, Democratic National Convention," 1964. Permission from Jacqueline Hamer Flakes.

Maya Angelou, "On the Pulse of Morning," 1993. Copyright © 1993 by Maya Angelou. Used by permission of Random House, an imprint and division of Penguin Random House LLC. All rights reserved.

Lorraine Hansberry, "The Black Revolution and the White Backlash," 1964. Permission to use copyrighted material granted by Joi Gresham, Literary Trustee, Lorraine Hansberry Properties Trust.

Audre Lorde, "Age, Race, Class, and Sex: Women Redefining Difference," 1980. Reprinted by Consent of Sheedy Lit.

Marian Wright Edelman, "Standing Up for the World's Children," 1996. Courtesy Marian Wright Edelman.

Barbara Lee, "Beyond Iraq, Beyond Haiti, and Beyond the Doctrine of Preemption," Courtesy Barbara Lee.

Carol Moseley Braun, "Announcement Speech for Democratic Nomination," 2003. Courtesy Carol Moseley Braun.

Ruby Nell Sales, "Can I Get a Witness?" 2017. Courtesy Ruby Nell Sales.

ABOUT THE AUTHOR

Janet Dewart Bell is a social justice activist with a doctorate in leadership and change from Antioch University. She founded the Derrick Bell Lecture on Race in American Society series at the New York University School of Law and is the author of *Lighting the Fires of Freedom: African American Women in the Civil Rights Movement* and the co-editor (with Vincent M. Southerland) of *Race, Rights, and Redemption: The Derrick Bell Lectures on the Law and Critical Race Theory* (both published by The New Press). The founder and president of LEAD Inter-Generational Solutions, Inc., as well as an award-winning television and radio producer, she lives in New York City.

PUBLISHING IN THE PUBLIC INTEREST

Thank you for reading this book published by The New Press; we hope you enjoyed it. New Press books and authors play a crucial role in sparking conversations about the key political and social issues of our day.

We hope that you will stay in touch with us. Here are a few ways to keep up to date with our books, events, and the issues we cover:

- Sign up at www.thenewpress.com/subscribe to receive updates on New Press authors and issues and to be notified about local events
- www.facebook.com/newpressbooks
- www.twitter.com/thenewpress
- www.instagram.com/thenewpress

Please consider buying New Press books not only for yourself, but also for friends and family and to donate to schools, libraries, community centers, prison libraries, and other organizations involved with the issues our authors write about.

The New Press is a 501(c)(3) nonprofit organization; if you wish to support our work with a tax-deductible gift please visit www.thenewpress.com/donate or use the QR code below.